A Guide *to the*

TEACHERS COLLEGE READING AND WRITING PROJECT

Classroom Libraries

Curated by

LUCY CALKINS ✦ NORAH MALLANEY
SHANA FRAZIN ✦ AND COLLEAGUES

Heinemann

DEDICATED TO TEACHERS™

Heinemann
361 Hanover Street
Portsmouth, NH 03801–3912
www.heinemann.com

Offices and agents throughout the world

© 2016 by Lucy Calkins

Library of Congress Cataloging-in-Publication Data is on file with the Library of Congress.

ISBN-13: 978-0-325-08975-1

Editors: Karen Kawaguchi and Tracy Wells
Production: Elizabeth Valway, David Stirling, and Abigail Heim
Cover and interior designs: Jenny Jensen Greenleaf
Photography: Peter Cunningham
Composition: Publishers' Design and Production Services, Inc.
Manufacturing: Steve Bernier

Printed in the United States of America on acid-free paper
23 22 21 20 19 B&B 4 5 6 7 8

Contents

Contributors
and
Consultants
from the Field

Teachers College Reading and Writing Project

The entire staff of the Teachers College Reading and Writing Project contributed to and supported the work on this vast curation project. Particular thanks go to:

Marissa Altamura, Project Coordinator

Carl Anderson, Staff Developer; speaker; author

Maggie Beattie Roberts, Lead Staff Developer; presenter; author and Units of Study for Teaching Writing series coauthor

Heather Burns, Staff Developer; former teacher and literacy coach

Lucy Calkins, Founding Director; Teachers College/Columbia University Robinson Professor of Children's Literature and Literacy Specialist Program co-director; leading literacy authority and keynote speaker; author or coauthor of numerous books, including the Units of Study for Teaching Reading/Writing series

Katie Clements, Staff Developer; Units of Study for Reading/Writing series author/coauthor

M. Colleen Cruz, Senior Lead Staff Developer; author; former teacher

Mary Ehrenworth, Deputy Director for Middle Schools; author; Units of Study for Teaching Reading/Writing series author/coauthor

Kimberly Fox, Staff Developer; former special education teacher; Units of Study series illustrator

Elizabeth Franco, Senior Research Associate; former teacher; Units of Study for Teaching Reading/Writing series author/coauthor/illustrator

Simone Fraser, Staff Developer; former upper grade elementary teacher

Shana Frazin, Staff Developer; Units of Study for Writing series coauthor

Brooke Geller, Senior Lead Staff Developer; Units of Study for Teaching Reading coauthor

Eric Hand, Staff Developer; former teacher

Kelly Boland Hohne, Writer in Residence, Senior Research Associate; Units of Study for Reading/Writing series author/coauthor

Norah Mallaney, Literacy Specialist (Grades 3–5); former teacher

Marjorie Martinelli, Senior Research Associate; co-director of Reading Rescue; "ChartChums" blogger; author and Units of Study for Teaching Reading/Writing series coauthor/illustrator

Michelle McGrath, Staff Developer; former teacher-researcher, mentor, and teacher

Heather Michael, Staff Developer (grades 6–8); Teachers College Curriculum and Teaching Doctoral program student; former teacher

Mary Ann Mustac, Executive Assistant

Mike Ochs, Staff Developer; Teachers College Literacy Specialist program; Units of Study for Teaching Reading/Writing series coauthor

Leah Bragin Page, Staff Developer; former general education and inclusion teacher and literacy coach

Molly Picardi, Staff Developer (Grades K–2); Teachers College Literacy Specialist program graduate student

Alissa Reicherter, Staff Developer; Units of Study for Teaching Reading series coauthor

Kate Roberts, Staff Developer; presenter; author and Units of Study for Teaching Writing series coauthor; former middle school teacher and literacy coach

Cynthia Satterlee, Staff Developer; former teacher

Emily Butler Smith, Senior Research Associate, Lead Staff Developer; Units of Study for Teaching Writing/Reading series coauthor

Kristin Smith, Staff Developer; Units of Study for Teaching Reading series coauthor; former teacher

Janet Steinberg, Research and Data Manager; Units of Study for Teaching Reading series coauthor; former literacy coach

Kathleen Tolan, Senior Deputy Director; Units of Study for Teaching Reading/Writing series author/coauthor

Katie Wears, Staff Developer; Units of Study for Teaching Reading series coauthor; former K–8 literacy coach

Pablo Wolfe, Staff Developer; former teacher

Children's Literature and Education/Literacy Experts

Richard Allington, Professor of Education, University of Tennessee; past president of IRA, NRC; editorial advisory board member for numerous scholarly education journals and publications; author

Alyson Beecher, "Kid Lit Frenzy" blogger

Kylene Beers, educational consultant; presenter; author

Lois Bridges, literacy publisher and editor, Scholastic; literacy specialist; former teacher and consultant

Katherine Bomer, educational consultant; teacher; author

Randy Bomer, literacy consultant; Professor, College of Education, University of Texas; author; TCRWP former co-director; past president of NCTE

David Booth, Professor Emeritus in Education, Coordinator of Elementary Programs at Ontario Institute for Studies in Education, University of Toronto; literacy consultant; speaker; author

Louise Cappizzo, "The Nonfiction Detectives" blogger

Betty Carter, Professor Emerita of Children's and Young Adult Literature, Texas Woman's University; former reading teacher and school librarian

Anna Gratz Cockerille, literacy consultant; "Two Writing Teachers" blogger and Heinemann blog editor; Units of Study in Teaching Writing coauthor; former TCRWP staff developer, Heinemann editor, and teacher

Kathy Collins, literacy consultant; presenter; author; former teacher

Smokey Daniels, literacy consultant; presenter; author; former teacher, teacher-educator, and editor

Diane DeFord, Professor, Language and Literacy Instruction and Teacher Education, University of Southern Carolina; author

Ralph Fletcher, literacy consultant; presenter; author

Judy Freeman, children's literature consultant and book reviewer; speaker; author

Don Futterman, Executive Director, Israel Center for Educational Innovation

Emily Gasoi, Senior Consultant, Artful Education; former teacher

Carrie Gelson, "There's a Book for That" blogger

Anne Goudvis, staff developer, Public Education and Business Coalition; literacy consultant; author; former teacher

Stephanie Harvey, literacy consultant; presenter; author; former Public Education and Business Coalition staff developer; former teacher

Georgia Heard, presenter; poet; author; former TCRWP senior staff developer

Ellin Keene, literacy consultant; presenter; author; former teacher, professor, and staff developer at the Public Education and Business Coalition

Penny Kittle, literacy consultant; presenter; author; teacher

Lester Laminack, Professor Emeritus, Western Carolina University; literacy and children's literature consultant; presenter; author

Alexandra Marron, former TCRWP senior research associate, staff developer, writer-in-residence; Units of Study for Teaching Reading/Writing series author/coauthor

Liz Rosado-McGrath, national content specialist, Heinemann Publishing; former teacher, EL specialist

Donalyn Miller, Grades 4–6 teacher; presenter; author

Heidi Mills, Professor, Department of Instruction and Teacher Education, University of South Carolina; founding member, Center for Inquiry; literacy consultant; presenter; author

Kate Montgomery, international literacy consultant; author; former editor and TCRWP lead researcher and teacher

Elizabeth Moore, literacy coach and consultant; "Two Writing Teachers" blogger; Units of Study in Reading/Teaching Writing series coauthor; former teacher and TCRWP staff developer

Kristine Mraz, educational consultant; author; teacher; "ChartChums" blogger; former TCRWP staff developer

The Nerdy Book Club online blog community

Cathy Potter, "The Nonfiction Detectives" blogger

Jen Serravallo, literacy consultant; presenter; author; former TCRWP staff developer and teacher

Anita Silvey, former editor-in-chief of *The Horn Book Magazine*; author

Pam Smith, national content specialist, Heinemann Publishing; educational consultant; former principal and teacher

Katherine Sokolowski, "Nerdy Book Club" and "Read, Write, Reflect" blogger

Elizabeth Sulzby, Professor of Education, University of Michigan; emergent literacy author and expert

Jim Trelease, author; former presenter

Gita Varadarajan, literacy coach and consultant

Jennifer Vincent, "Teach Mentor Texts" blogger

Judy Wallis, staff development and literacy consultant; author; former teacher, literacy coach, and university instructor

Joe Yukish, educational consultant; presenter; author; former TCRWP Director, Senior Primary Reading Adviser, and Reading Recovery professor

Teachers and Librarians

Alyssa Agoston, Grade 1 teacher, Elms Elementary School, Jackson, NJ

Rebecca Anderson, media center clerk, Las Virgenes Unified School District, Calabasas, CA

Christa Anderson, literacy leader, Middleton-Cross Plains Area School District, Middleton, WI

Barbara Andrews, literacy specialist, Las Virgenes Unified School District, Calabasas, CA

Lisa Badalamenti, reading specialist, NYC Board of Education, New York, NY

Lindsay Barna, literacy content area specialist and coach, Piscataway Township Schools, Piscataway, NJ

Jennifer Barnes, Grades K–1 teacher, Center for Inquiry, Richland County School District Two, Columbia, SC

Amanda Blake, Grades 4–5 teacher, Center for Inquiry, Richland County School District Two, Columbia, SC

Karan Bliske, teacher, Marshall Public Schools, Marshall, WI

Sarah Boland, special education teacher, George G. White Middle School, Hillsdale, NJ

Susan Bolte, Grades K–1 teacher, Center for Inquiry, Richland County School District Two, Columbia, SC

Kristen Bourn, teacher, ISG American School of Jubail, Saudi Arabia

Nancy Boyd, librarian, East Hills School, Roslyn, NY

Nancy Bradley, instructional coach, Exley Elementary School, Katy, TX

Tameka Breland, Grades 4–5 teacher, Center for Inquiry, Richland County School District Two, Columbia, SC

Kristen Brennan, instructional coach, Bonnie Holland Elementary School, Katy, TX

Patricia Bryan, Grade 6 teacher, English East Side Community School, New York, NY

Sonja Cherry-Paul, teacher, Farragut Middle School, Hastings-on-Hudson, NY; professional development consultant; author

Michele Ciconte, Grade 2 teacher, Tatnall School, Wilmington, DE

Jaleelah Cooke, principal, and the entire staff at PS 369, Brooklyn, NY

Marija Crosson, Grade 4 teacher, Mastery Charter Schools, Philadelphia, PA

Elizabeth Culkin, principal, PS 176, New York, NY

Deb Dagitz, library media specialist, Elm Lawn Elementary School, Middleton, WI

Jenni Darby-Lanker, teacher, Gresham-Barlow School District, Portland, OR

Nicole Dixon, Grade 7 ELA teacher, Eastside Community School, New York, NY

Tomi Dodson, Grade 2 teacher, Stephens Elementary School, Houston, TX

Justin Dolci, ELA teacher, Jefferson County Public Schools, Louisville, KY

Kitty Donohoe, teacher, Santa Monica, CA

Brenna Dorgan, Grade 4 teacher, Stephens Elementary School, Houston, TX

Kathy Doyle, retired teacher; former teacher-pilot for TCRWP and Units of Study series

Dina Ercolano, principal, PS 158, New York, NY

Sonhando Estwick, principal, Tompkins Square Middle School, New York, NY

Rebecca Fagin, principal, PS 29, New York, NY

Stacey Fell, teacher, Tompkins Square Middle School, New York, NY; Units of Study for Teaching Writing series coauthor

Michelle Fiorini, teacher, Benjamin Middle School, West Chicago, IL

Lauren Fontana, principal, PS 6, New York, NY

Gina Fontana, curriculum specialist and literacy coach, LCC Day School, St. Petersburg, FL

Brandon Foote, Grades 2–3 teacher, Center for Inquiry, Richland County School District Two, Columbia, SC

Laurie Foote, teacher, North Clackamas School District, Milwaukie, OR

Ben Frazell, instructional coach, Inspired Teaching Public Charter School, Washington, DC

Tracey Fritch, Grade 6 ELA teacher, Springton Lake Middle School, Media, PA

Liza Garza, bilingual programs instructional officer, Katy Independent School District, Katy, TX

Mary Catherine Gregorio, Grade 4 teacher, Millstone River School, Plainsboro, NJ

Matt Halpern, K–5 literacy strategist, Regional School Unit 5, Freeport, ME

Stephanie Hardinger, Grades 4–5 lead teacher, East Palo Alto Charter School, Aspire Public Schools, Palo Alto, CA

Jade Hargrave, Grade 1 teacher, Nathaniel Morton Elementary, Plymouth, MA

Marie Hartney, Middle School ELA teacher, LCC Day School, St. Petersburg, FL

Chris Hass, Grades 2–3 teacher, Center for Inquiry, Richland County School District Two, Columbia, SC

Heathcote Elementary School teachers, Scarsdale, NY

Carrie Hepburn, elementary ELA content leader, Francis Howell School District, Saint Charles, MO

Allison Hepfer, teacher, Bethlehem Central School District, Glenmont, NY

Erin Hermann, literacy specialist/coach, Colchester Elementary School, Colchester, CT

Kaitlyn Holloway, Grade 1 teacher, Elms Elementary School, Jackson, NJ

Stephanie Jackson, teacher, Twin Falls School District, Idaho Falls, ID

Alyna Jacobs, principal, South Mountain Elementary School, South Orange, NJ

Dana Johansen, Grade 5 English teacher, Greenwich Academy, Greenwich, CT; presenter; author

Juliana Johnson, K–3 curriculum and instruction teacher resource specialist, West Windsor-Plainsboro Regional School District; West Windsor, NJ

Scott Johnson, Grades 4–5 teacher, Center for Inquiry, Richland County School District Two; Columbia, SC

Alicia Felts Jones, instructional content facilitator, Union County Public Schools, Monroe, NC

Jasmine Junsay, teacher, PS 29, New York, NY

Renee Keeler, teacher, grade 3, Lee Elementary School, Los Alamitos, CA

Melissa Klosterman, Grades K–1 teacher, Center for Inquiry, Richland County School District Two, Columbia, SC

Sandy Kope, teacher, grade 1, Canyon Creek Elementary, Bothell, WA

Peter Kornicker, librarian; PS 161, New York, NY

Kristen Kowalick, Kindergarten teacher, John Hancock Demonstration Elementary School, Philadelphia, PA

Stephanie Kramer, teacher, Menahga Public Schools, Menahga, MN

Lisa Lane, assistant principal, Jackson School District, Jackson, NJ

Jennifer Latimer, school media specialist, Clinton Elementary School, Maplewood, NJ

Michael Lewis, Grade 5 teacher, Deer Hill School, Cohasset, MA; Apple Distinguished Educator; author

Ginny Lockwood, principal, Mamaroneck Avenue School, Mamaroneck, NY

Deborah Longo, preK site coordinator, Targee Street Pre-K Center, New York, NY

Allison Lucchesi, Grade 4 teacher, E.M. Baker School, Great Neck, NY

Adam Marcus, librarian, PS 32K, New York, NY

Maria Maroni, teacher, Stow-Munroe Falls Schools, Stow-Munroe, OH

Cindy Marten, superintendent, San Diego Unified School District; literacy specialist; author

Carole Mashamesh, Grade 7 humanities teacher, Tompkins Square Middle School, New York, NY

Gianna Matchniff, Grade 1 teacher, Heron Heights Elementary School, Parkland, FL

Casey Maxwell, Kindergarten teacher, PS 446, New York, NY

Lynne McCune, literacy specialist, Colchester Public Schools, Colchester, CT

Monica McDearmon, Grade 6 teacher, Chickahominy Middle School, Mechanicsville, VA

Medea McEvoy, principal, PS 267, New York, NY

Jenna McMahon, Grades 1–2 teacher, Kiel School, Kinnelon, NJ

Jessie Miller, ELA and SS curriculum coordinator, Katy Independent School District, Katy, TX

Kate Mills, teacher, grade 4, Knollwood Elementary School, Fair Haven, NJ

Stacey Moore, curriculum coach, Van Buren School District, Van Buren, AR

Bridget Mullett, teacher, Pitner Elementary School, Acworth, GA

Tim O'Keefe, Grades 2–3 teacher, Center for Inquiry, Richland County School District Two, Columbia, SC

Patricia O'Rourke, Grade 2 teacher, ReNEW Schools Charter Management Organization, New Orleans, LA

Jill Osmerg, curriculum support teacher, Woodland Elementary School, Sandy Springs, GA

Tiffany Palmtier, Grades K–1 teacher, Center for Inquiry, Richland County School District Two, Columbia, SC

Danielle Parella, Grade 1 teacher, Elms Elementary School, Jackson, NJ

Meredith-Leigh Pleasants, instructional coach, ReNEW Schools Charter Management Organization, New Orleans, LA

Jennifer Rodman Priddy, Grade 4 teacher, St. Paul's School, Brooklandville, MD

PS 6 teachers, New York, NY

PS 29 teachers, New York, NY

PS 59 teachers, New York, NY

PS 158 teachers, New York, NY

PS 176 teachers, New York, NY

PS 267 teachers, New York, NY

Jeny Randall, teacher, language arts/intermediate and upper science, Saratoga Independent School, Saratoga Springs, NY

Lisa Raney, Grade 2 teacher, Elms Elementary School, Jackson, NJ

Miriam Regan, Kindergarten teacher, Schaumburg Elementary ReNEW Charter School, New Orleans, LA

Rachel Reilly, Grade 2 teacher, Sharon Elementary School, Robbinsville, NJ

Brooke Rennie, Grade 8 ELA teacher, The Learning Community Charter School, Central Falls, RI

Kelli Rich, teacher, Mason City Schools, Mason City, OH

Marni Rogers, literacy coach, Gwinnett County Public Schools, Gwinnett, GA

Laura Salopek, reading teacher, Deforest Middle School, Deforest, WI

Donna Santman, academic director, Harlem Village Academies, New York, NY; educational consultant; author; former TCRWP staff developer

Adele Schroeder, principal, PS 59, New York, NY

Denise Schweikart, literacy coach, Greenwood School District 50, Greenwood, SC

Michele Shipman, assistant principal, Van Buren School District, Van Buren, AR

Gillian Shotwell, instructional coach, PS 249, New York, NY

Josephine Sinagra, teacher, PS 139, New York, NY

Valerie Stanley, teacher, Lyon County School District, Yerington, NV

Elisabeth Stephens and her class, Grade 5 teacher, PS 29, New York, NY

Kim Stieber-White, library media specialist, Glacier Creek Middle School, Cross Plains, WI

Maria R. Stile, principal, Heathcote Elementary School, Scarsdale, NY

Kate Sweeney, library media specialist, J. O. Wilson Elementary School, Washington, DC

Andrea Swenson, librarian, Eastside Middle School, New York, NY

Melanie Swider, literacy coach, Simsbury Schools, Simsbury, CT

Lori Talish, teacher/librarian, PS 59, New York, NY

Robyn Thomas, Grades PreK–2 lead learning coach, Mason City Schools, Mason City, OH

Tompkins Square Middle School teachers, New York, NY

Caryn Alexander Tsagalis, Grade 1 teacher, Cherokee Elementary School, Lake Forest, IL

Rachel Venegas, Kindergarten teacher, E.M. Baker School, Great Neck, NY

Aimee Volk, Grade 3 teacher, Kreamer Street Elementary School, Patchogue, NY

Kristen Robbins Warren, Grades 7–8 ELA teacher, NYC Department of Education; "A Kind of a Library" blogger

Jenny Weber, teacher, Horace Mann Elementary School, Washington, DC

Nora Wentworth, teacher, Akili Academy, New Orleans, LA

Emily Whitecotton, Grades 4–5 teacher, Center for Inquiry, Richland County School District Two, Columbia, SC

Deb Zaffiro, instructional coach, Greenfield Public Schools, Greenfield, WI

Teachers College, Columbia University

Alicia Andres-Arroyo, graduate student

Rebecca Bellingham, Professor of Education

Alice Day Brown, graduate student

Ellen Ellis, Professor of Education

Karen Finnerty, graduate student

Nicole Fristachi, Administrative Assistant

Maria Paula Ghiso, Assistant Professor of Literacy Education

Ed Hodson, graduate student

Noel Imbriale, graduate student

Maria Souto Manning, Associate Professor of Early Childhood Education

Elizabeth Massi, graduate student

Vincent Phram, graduate student

Laura Schwartz, graduate student

Marjorie Siegel, Professor of Education

Jennifer Snyder, graduate student

Brittania Surles, graduate student

Publishers, Bookstores, Book Clubs, and Suppliers

ABDO Publishing

Abrams Books

Albert Whitman & Company

American Girl Publishing

Arbordale Publishing

Arte Publico Press

Bank Street Bookstore, NYC

Barefoot Books

Barron's Educational Series

Bearport Publishing

Bellwether Media

Blueberry Hill Books

Bookmasters

Books of Wonder

Booksource: Special thanks to Michelle Abeln, Cheryl Dickemper, Diona Graves, and
    Brandi Ivester, collection development specialists

Brilliance Publishing (Amazon.com)

Candlewick Press

Capstone Publishing

Charlesbridge Publishing

Chronicle Books

Cinco Puntos Press

Crabtree Publishing

Creston Books

Cricket Books

Dawn Publications

DK Eyewitness Books (Penguin Random House)

Eerdmans

Enslow Publishers

Firefly Books

Flying Start Books

Hachette Book Group

Hameray Publishing

HarperCollins Children's Books

HarperCollins

Heinemann

Holiday House Books

Houghton Mifflin Harcourt

House of Anansi Press (Groundwood)

Hyperion Books

Independent Publishers Group

Kaeden Books

Kids Can Press

Kirkus Review

Ko Kids Books

Lee & Low Books

Lerner Publishing Group

Macmillan Publishers

Mary Ruth Books

McSweeney's Quarterly & Books

Microcosm Publishing

Midpoint Publishing

Mighty Media Press

Milkweed Editions

National Geographic Kids

National Geographic Partners

National Geographic Society

Okapi Educational Publishing

Orca Book Publishers

Owlkids Books

PeachTree Publishers

Penguin Books

Penguin Random House

Perseus Books Group

Pioneer Valley Books

Publisher's Group Worldwide

Random House Kids

Reading Reading Books

Richard C. Owen Publishers

RiverStream Publishing

Rosen Publishing

Saddleback Educational Publishing

Saunders Book Company

Scholastic

Seedling Resources (Continental Press)

Shelter Publications

Silver Dolphin Books

Simon & Schuster

Sourcebooks

Stenhouse Publishers

Sterling Publishing

Sundance Publishing

Tanglewood Press

Teacher Created Materials

Toon Books

Top Shelf Productions

Townsend Press

Trinity University Press

Web of Life Children's Books

Workman Publishing

A Note of Special Thanks

We are grateful to everyone who offered time or expertise to the Classroom Libraries project, but we would like to extend special thanks to the following individuals whose contributions were particularly crucial to its success: Alicia Andres-Arroyo, David Booth, Heather Burns, Kathy Doyle, Karen Finnerty, Abby Heim, Noel Imbriale, Jasmine Junsay, Penny Kittle, Michael Lewis, Heidi Mills, Tim O'Keefe, Leah Bragin Page, Vincent Phram, Laura Schwartz, Jennifer Snyder, Teachers of NYC PS 6, Teachers of NYC PS 158, Teachers of Heathcote Elementary School, Julia Tolan, Pablo Wolfe, and Joe Yukish.

Chapter 1

Letter to Teachers

Dear Teachers,

For the Teachers College Reading and Writing Project (TCRWP), this effort to create Classroom Libraries has been an all-important mission: to build state-of-the-art Classroom Libraries filled with awe-inspiring, spine-tingling, mind-bending books that deeply engage students, strengthen reading and thinking skills, and inspire kids to become lifelong readers.

As I write this letter, I'm trying to picture who you are, where you are. I like to think that you are opening a giant box filled to the brim with the Teachers College Reading and Writing Project Classroom Library you have ordered, or perhaps one or more shelves to begin or continue growing your Classroom Library, and that this *Guide* lies on the top of the books, serving as an introduction to that library.

The shelves in the boxes you are opening were curated by the entire staff of the Teachers College Reading and Writing Project. We combined our ideas with those of other reading and literature experts, teachers, librarians, and students, to thoughtfully collect, examine, and select books—books that will make a difference in the lives of students as readers and learners.

The TCRWP Classroom Libraries were created in a way that is worlds apart from how most other libraries are created. The Classroom Libraries Project began with our scouring the world to find the best literacy coaches, top experts in teaching reading and writing, renowned librarians, and mentor teachers who love books. Then we asked those experts to join our cause. We reached out to respected pros on children's and young adult literature as well, soliciting book recommendations from everyone. We got recommendations from people you know—Katherine and Randy Bomer, David Booth, Lois Bridges, Ralph Fletcher, Maria Paula Ghiso, Stephanie Harvey, Lester Laminack, Mariana Souto Manning, Heidi Mills, Betty Carter, Anita Silvey, people from the Nerdy Book Club, all of our own staff and from hundreds of literacy coaches, authors, and teachers. We explained to each of the people that we approached that for TCRWP, this is a mission of love. All the profits TCRWP gets from this will be plowed back into an ongoing effort to provide kids with the best possible Classroom Libraries.

Eventually we had lists of recommendations from hundreds of experts—a total of more than 22,000 books, recommended for readers in grades 3–8 (more books were recommended for the younger grades). We then got copies of each of these books. All of us at TCRWP worked tirelessly for half a year in a gigantic basement—inventorying, leveling, reviewing, and curating shelves. For every book that we selected, there were scores of others that we set aside.

This, then, is what sets this work apart from other classroom libraries made by lone teachers, or created by a few people at a book distributor or a publisher (which are often limited to the books that publisher puts out or has bought the rights to).

Also, these Classroom Libraries are not the good-for-you, cod-liver-oil sort of libraries. Much as we loved *Jane Eyre* and *Anne of Green Gables*, neither is here. Time-honored classics are included, but many books are the cutting-edge, imaginative titles that kids today will love—the Harry Potter series, the *Fault in Our Stars*, the *Diary of a Wimpy Kid*, the *Wonder*, the Don't Let the Pigeon series, the *Invention-of-the-Super-Soaker* books, the *I Survived* kinds of books. We carefully chose books based on students' interests and on the richness of the books, looking for books that could be mined again and again. We also looked for quality of writing and content, and for a diverse range of genres, topics, and author styles.

Just for a moment, think about the astronomical amounts of money this nation has spent over the last decade to diagnose and "cure" reading deficiencies. Think of the billions of dollars worth of tests that are constantly developed to ferret out students' deficits. Think of how readers (and teachers) have been blamed and shamed in the public square. Think of the resources poured into developing worksheets and software programs that make kids detest reading. None of that has turned students into readers. None of that has done the job that Harry Potter and Captain Underpants have done!

My colleagues and I think of the TCRWP Classroom Libraries as a statement to politicians and policy makers, educational leaders, and the rest. *This* is what kids need to become readers. Not those tests, not those programs, not those skills and drills—but amazing, thrilling *books*.

We laugh at memories of our early efforts to supply our own classrooms with libraries. Most of us remember walking into a bare room in August—and staring at those near-empty bookshelves. We remember that frantic feeling when we had to fill our shelves with *something*. Norah went to a public library, filling a milk crate with *any* book that seemed remotely within reach for her students. Shana dug out musty copies of *National Geographic* magazines to substitute for books. Molly Picardi (one of the K–2 library curators) raced around a book warehouse sale, piling out-of-date books into bags—$20 per bag. Of course, this effort to move heaven and earth to provide students with books has become part of what it means to be a teacher.

But the truth is that scooping any book from warehouse shelves is no way to provision a classroom with the one single resource that will make the biggest difference in students' lives as learners. Think of it this way. Would you dream of teaching *math* by scooping up any ol' picked-over math books from rummage sales and warehouse closings? Not a chance. Instead, you'd bring together the professionals who love math and know it deeply. You'd ask them to help you research approaches to math. You'd search high and low for books that could help you teach math in clear, compelling, research-based ways. Teaching literacy deserves at least as much!

Think about the number of students who hate to read. A study by the American Library Association showed that when asked, the day before graduating from high school, "Will you voluntarily pick up a book after graduation?" 85% of America's kids said, "No way." And that is 85% of the kids who stayed in school long enough to graduate—another huge group dropped out long before graduation!

If you and I had to select all our books from leftover remnants, wouldn't we also be turned off from reading? Considering what we've all been through as teachers, we're flabbergasted there hasn't been more talk and more work over the past few decades around developing high-quality classroom libraries. We think the mission of the Classroom Library Project to put heart-stopping, gut-wrenching, glorious books into the hands of our students is critical. We believe that once these libraries reach children's hands, nothing on earth can *keep* them from reading.

Chapter 4 of this *Guide* ("What's in the TCRWP Classroom Libraries?"), will provide more information about our process of curating these libraries. You'll hear that many of the books we selected function like that gray cardigan or blue tie in your wardrobe that can be mixed and matched to fit with lots of different outfits. That is, many books have been included because they can do quadruple duty. For instance, a book can serve as high-interest fiction, merit close interpretive reading, lend itself to rich thematic analysis, and fit neatly alongside other titles in a social issues book club. Many books are nested alongside others. For example, we often include at least two biographies about the same person, with one being more accessible than another. This allows the one biography to provide readers with the prior knowledge that will help them read the more complex text.

A geography shelf is layered, with books that bring each continent to life by capturing the geography, weather, landscape, and plants of that continent. Then, for each continent, there are books that spotlight two distinctly different communities within that continent. All of that information can then be related to books about life—schools, food, ethnic traditions—within those places.

In a similar fashion, we selected several historical fiction books about a particular era at each level of text complexity, and have included a nonfiction text or two about that historical era.

We generally include only three or four books from a series, including usually two copies of the first book in the series. We know that once a reader is hooked into a series, you can help that reader find additional volumes within the school or public library.

Although you and your school system have spent a fair sum on these collections, even the complete libraries are designed as "starter" sets. You will need more books. But the good news is that you and your students will have the momentum and the energy to get those books. Your students will be willing to write petitions, make and sell bead necklaces and bookmarks, wrap books at a local bookstore, invest in their own online bookseller accounts—*anything* to continue developing their library.

Because these Classroom Libraries have been carefully structured, I expect that as you secure more books, you'll fill out and extend the existing structure. You and your students might find other books for a nonfiction topic-based subcategory such as "Cool Careers." You may suggest that a new category—perhaps "Extreme, Strange, and Odd Animals"—be added to your nonfiction library. Your students might announce that the shelf, "If you liked *Hunger Games*, you will like . . ." needs new additions. (See Chapter 3, "Setting Up, Introducing, and Managing Your Classroom Library," for information about the tools for TCRWP Classroom Libraries, including book bin labels.)

As you prepare to set up your new Classroom Library, we hope you'll consult this *Guide* to help you and your students get oriented, as well as provide guidance on organizing and making the best use of your new library. In this *Guide*, you'll find discussions on topics including:

■ the research base for the development of the Classroom Libraries

■ how to set up, introduce, and manage your library

■ the content of shelves and how books were selected

■ assessment, leveling of books, and matching books to readers

■ overviews of teaching methods for reading aloud, independent reading, conferring and small-group work, partnerships, and book clubs.

Richard Allington, past president of the International Reading Association, has written and spoken often about the three things that readers need to flourish: access to books they find fascinating, protected time to read, and expert instruction. We hope these libraries will provide you and your students with the first of these, will inspire you to protect the second, and allow you to focus on the third.

—*Lucy Calkins*

Chapter 2

Research Base for the TCRWP Classroom Libraries

As students become engaged readers, they provide themselves with self-generated learning opportunities that are equivalent to several years of education.

<small>(GUTHRIE AND WIGFIELD 2000)</small>

The books in the Teachers College Reading and Writing Project Classroom Libraries represent a big investment. People may ask, "How does one know if it's worth it—investing in books, like this? What's the research base for this decision?"

The truth is that the research base is so deep, so thorough, and so long-standing that anyone who works in reading knows that investing in books is a wise choice. If the goal is to support growth in reading, there are few decisions that will have more payoff than the decision to give students access to high-quality and high-interest fiction and nonfiction.

A recent study that has been highly influential is a global study instigated by the International Literacy Association (formerly the International Reading Association). The ILA tasked a team of researchers to investigate the relationship between students' reading engagement and their academic success, as measured by the Programme for International Student Assessment (PISA) exam and also by grade point averages. The PISA exam measures an extremely high level of literacy—the kind of higher-order thinking and critical, analytical reading that we most want all our students to be skilled at.

This ILA study found that "attitude toward reading, frequency of leisure reading, and diversity of reading materials" were critical variables in not just reading achievement, but also academic achievement as measured by grade point averages (Brozo, Shiel, and Topping 2011, 311).

What was fascinating about this study is how reading for pleasure mitigated benefits and disadvantages of income. "Youth from the lowest socioeconomic status (SES) who were highly engaged readers performed as well on the assessments as highly engaged youth from the middle SES group" (308). In fact, using regression analysis, the ILA study suggests that "keeping students engaged in reading and learning might make it possible for them to overcome what might otherwise be insuperable barriers to academic success" (308).

Creating opportunities for students to become engaged readers, it turns out, is a great tool of social justice. The sad truth is that many kids are growing up in this country with little or no access to books in their communities. In concentrated-poverty communities, the situation is especially dire. A recent study by Susan Neuman and Naomi Moland found that in Anacostia, a low-income neighborhood in Washington, D.C., not a single preschool-level book was available for sale, and stores in that neighborhood carried only five books for children in grades K–12—only one age-appropriate book for every 830 kids; that in sharp contrast

to middle-income communities, where Neuman found in a 2001 study that there were 13 books available for each and every child in one middle-income Philadelphia neighborhood. With "book deserts" in many communities in this nation, it becomes even more urgent to give kids access to a plentiful supply of high-quality and high-interest books to support their reading lives.

Guthrie and Wigfield (2000) reinforce the significance of students reading fiction and nonfiction for pleasure, showing that the amount of knowledge students gain from this kind of reading has a tremendous effect on all their academic achievement. Their study demonstrated that, "as students become engaged readers, they provide themselves with self-generated learning opportunities that are equivalent to several years of education" (404). Engagement in reading, according to Guthrie and Wigfield, "may substantially compensate for low family income and poor educational background" (404). It makes sense. The more kids read, the more they know. The more they know, the more background knowledge they bring to their studies. The more they engage in content studies, the more they want to extend their reading.

Understanding the enormous impact that reading engagement has on academic success leads to the question of how to improve that engagement. Classroom libraries that offer a wide range of book choice can have a significant impact on improving reading motivation. As Richard Allington puts it, "students read more, understand more, and are more likely to continue reading when they have the opportunity to choose what they read" (2012a, 10). Allington points to a meta-analysis by Guthrie and Humenick, which found that the two most powerful factors for "increasing reading motivation and comprehension were (1) student access to many books and (2) personal choice of what to read" (Allington 2012a; Guthrie and Humenick 2004). Another recent study has shown that children's favorite books are the ones they choose on their own. The kids (ages six to seventeen) in this study tended to finish reading their books through to the end (*Kids & Family Reading Report* by Scholastic Inc. and YouGov [2014]).

Giving students the opportunity to learn to choose wisely from a wide variety of books inside the classroom also helps them to choose appropriate texts outside the classroom. This is a skill that Allington and his colleagues show "dramatically increases the likelihood that they will read outside of school" (Allington 2012a; Ivey and Broaddus 2001). Investing in books for children, then, is an investment in their growth during their tenure in school and beyond.

There is one sobering note that appears again and again in national and global studies around reading. Boys in every country demonstrate, overall, lower levels of reading engagement (Brozo, Shiel, and Topping 2011; Donahue, Daane, and Grigg 2003). The good news is that books such as graphic novels, fantasy, and adventure books show an immediate impact on motivating reluctant readers (Brozo 2002; Schwartz 2002; Schwartz 2010).

When you look at the books included in these classroom libraries, you'll see a strong emphasis on engaging titles. Teaching these readers strategies isn't going to be effective unless they actually choose to read. As the National Reading Panel puts it, "the importance of reading as an avenue to improved reading has been stressed by theorists, researchers, and practitioners alike, no matter what their perspectives. There are few ideas more widely accepted than that reading is learned through reading" (2000).

REFERENCES

Allington, R. 2012a. "Every Child, Every Day." *Educational Leadership* 69: 6, 10–15.
———. 2012b. *What Really Matters for Struggling Readers: Designing Research-Based Programs* (3rd ed.). Boston: Allyn and Bacon.
Brozo, W. G. 2002. *To Be a Boy, to Be a Reader: Engaging Teen and Preteen Boys in Active Literacy*. Newark, DE: International Reading Association.
Brozo, W. G., G. Shiel, and K. Topping. 2008/reissued online 2011. "Engagement in Reading: Lessons Learned from Three PISA Countries." *Journal of Adolescent & Adult Literacy* 51: 4, 304–15.
Donahue, P., M. Daane, and W. Grigg. 2003. *The Nation's Report Card: Reading Highlights 2003*. Washington, DC: National Center for Education Statistics.
Guthrie, J. T., and N. M. Humenick. 2004. "Motivating Students to Read: Evidence for Classroom Practices that Increase Motivation and Achievement." In P. McCardle and V. Chhabra (Eds.), *The Voice of Evidence in Reading Research* (329–54). Baltimore: Paul Brookes.
Guthrie, J. T., and A. Wigfield. 2000. "Engagement and Motivation in Reading." In M. L. Kamil, P. Mosenthal, P. D. Pearson, and R. Barr (Eds.), *Handbook of Reading Research* (Vol. 3, 403–22). Mahwah, NJ: Erlbaum.
Ivey, G., and K. Broaddus. 2001. "Just Plain Reading: A Survey of What Makes Students Want to Read in Middle School." *Reading Research Quarterly* 36, 350–77.
National Reading Panel. 2000. *Teaching Children to Read: An Evidence-Based Assessment of the Scientific Research Literature on Reading and Its Implications*

for Reading Instruction. Rockville, MD: National Institutes of Child Health and Human Development.

Neuman, S. B. and D. Celano. 2001."Access to Print in Low-Income and Middle-Income Communities: An Ecological Study of Four Neighborhoods." *Reading Research Quarterly* 36 (1): 8–26.

Neuman, S. B., D. Celano, and N. Moland. 2016. "Book Deserts: The Consequences of Income Segregation on Children's Access to Print." *Urban Education* 0042085916654525, first published on July 5, 2016 as doi:10.1177 /0042085916654525.

Scholastic Inc. and YouGov. 2014. *Kids & Family Reading Report.* scholastic.com /readingreport

Schwartz, G. E. 2002. "Graphic Novels for Multiple Literacies." *Journal of Adolescent & Adult Literacy* 46, 262–65.

———. 2010. "Graphic Novels, New Literacies, and Good Old Social Justice." *The Alan Review* Summer, 71–75.

Chapter 3

Setting Up, Introducing, and Managing Your Classroom Library

Making Your Classroom Library Inviting for Kids

The design of your classroom will send a powerful message to all who enter. Many teachers choose to devote a corner of the classroom to the library, wrapping bookshelves around an area that is also used for whole-class meetings and instruction such as that done in minilessons. The position of your library can convey the message, "This classroom is a place where books and reading are treasured."

You'll want to move heaven and earth to make your classroom library into an inviting place. When I was a first-year teacher, just before the school year began, I was inspired to visit a local sawmill, where I found the most gigantic stump imaginable. I convinced the people at that sawmill to cut the giant stump in half, and somehow, I got those gigantic stump halves into my classroom, using them to frame the classroom library. My stumps are still there, thirty years later, helping a teacher say to kids, "This corner of the room is a special place."

Teachers may use stumps, couches, pillows, or low mood lighting to make the classroom library into an inviting place. Taking lessons from favorite bookstores, teachers may group similar titles, with fantasy books in one section and biographies in another, or display favorite books with eye-catching covers facing out. Those books almost beg to be taken home, just as Corduroy sitting on the shelf at the store seemed to be waiting for Lisa to come and declare him to be hers for life.

Over time, you'll probably want to label shelves with signs such as, "If you loved *Wonder*, check out these titles!" We'll discuss those categories in much more detail later in this chapter.

Introducing Your Classroom Library to Kids at the Start of the Year

Start the year by gathering your kids into the inviting, special library you've set up. Announce to them, "We'll meet here often in the library. Can you see that

it's a really important place? See how the bookshelves are arranged. It is like we're wrapped in books—and that is what this year will be like. We are so lucky to have a library like this in our classroom. It's our greatest treasure."

Then again, to develop the biggest possible drumroll around your Classroom Library, you might decide to keep it off limits for a bit, channeling kids to read from tubs of books until they are ready to give the library its due, and then making an even bigger deal of the library. Some teachers wrap ribbon around the library until it is ready to be opened and then host a ribbon-cutting ceremony for the official opening.

Either way, you'll want to emphasize the role the classroom library will play in your students' reading lives. You might give a mini keynote address, saying, "You are going to love reading this year—every one of you will. The books in our library aren't just any ol' books. These are books that hundreds and hundreds of teachers, plus kids from all over the world, chose—and they chose these particular books by thinking about just one big thing. They asked themselves, 'What books will make kids *love* reading?'

You could continue, "So the books in this library aren't here because some old-fashioned Literature Expert announced, 'This will be *Good for You*'—like spinach is good for you. These books aren't the 'famous books that kids will probably hate' type books. No, these are the books that kids described saying, 'I know it sounds crazy, but I actually couldn't put that book down. I started reading it and forgot what time it was. My friend is reading it now, and I'm trying to get the next book by that same author.'"

You could also tell your kids, "These books are not all stories. Some books will teach you totally cool things, such as helping you imagine jobs you've never dreamed of, like hurricane hunters, acrobats, and spies. Then there are books about the grossest, most disgusting things, like bloodsuckers and fish farts. And books about topics that kids know a ton about and most grown-ups know nothing about. You'll find yourself dropping little facts into conversations about the projectile jaws of sharks, and people will look up and think, 'Are you a genius?'"

As important as fanfare is, it will also be important for you to teach children about the content and the organizational structure of the library. In the process of developing the TCRWP Classroom Libraries, we visited scores of classrooms to learn about students' preferences. What books did they especially like? What library sections mattered most? We were surprised to find that many students often didn't know the breadth of their own classroom libraries, and just stuck with a favorite part of the library.

Later in this *Guide*, you'll read about the logic that informed each shelf of the libraries. Some of that information might be important to share with your students.

Many teachers find it is important to give their students library tours, just as one would lead a tour in an art museum, showing off some of the most precious portions. You might also consider ways to communicate information to kids' families, such as sending home a letter to introduce the Classroom Library and how kids will benefit from it, or inviting family members to library tours led by you and your students.

The TCRWP Classroom Libraries come complete with tools to help you and your students organize and manage your library and to read with greater interest and depth. Bin labels such as "Lovable Pet Stories," "Adventure and Danger in History," and "LOL!" help organize enticing groupings of books. Small stickers displaying levels and the bin-card illustrations can be applied to individual books at the teacher's discretion, to support students' ability to independently select and reshelve books. Students can use "reviewer" sticky notes as close reading lenses that say what great readers may think as they read, like —"This feels symbolic" or "Stereotype alert!" The Post-its can help them prepare for book discussions and can be left behind to help future readers.

Imbue Your Classroom Culture with a Love of Books

Culture matters. Hang out with kids in the cafeteria, on the playground. Do this in your school and then in another school, and it will be immediately clear that in each school and classroom, a culture gets established among the student peer group, and that culture wields an incalculable force.

Just as some schools are saturated with an ethic of kindness and others are quite the opposite, so, too, there are "book cultures" in some schools where kids collect, swap, and trade books as if they are the Pokémon cards of long ago (while in other schools, kids worry that they'll be ostracized if they are seen with a book).

Your mission: to put books into your kids' hands and hearts.

Your Classroom Library is your most important way to grow a positive book culture and to recruit students to love reading, just as you do. You and your library have a mission: to put books into your kids' hands . . . and hearts. Your library will help your kids *want* to read and give them access to books. So you will want to develop ways in which the library can be part of an overall classroom culture that inspires kids to read.

Jerry Harste once said, "I see our job as teachers as creating a richly literate world in our classrooms, and then inviting kids to role play their way into being the readers and writers we long for them to become." There is something to Harste's idea that we simply forge ahead, making the classroom and the school into a place imbued with a reverence for books. Then we *act* as if students love books as we do. In such an environment, students can step into the roles of being strong, passionate readers and writers.

You may find it helps to also provide kids with the tools that help them assume the role of being avid readers. As mentioned above, the Classroom Libraries include tools such as Post-its for kids to leave inside a book's cover, telling the next reader, "Feels kinda boring at first, but hang in there, it gets really good" or "I nominate

this as best book on . . ." or "Bad cover—great book." Imagine reading along in this book and coming upon a page with a sticky note that says, "This is deep! Help me out!" You'd read that page with extra care. You might even seek out the note-writer to talk it over, and suddenly reading would become a social experience.

To create a book culture in your classroom, you'll want to give book talks that are almost like mini-commercials. Be sure to promote books that match your readers' current abilities.

"Friends, I must tell you about a book that I could not put down! I'm yawning today because I read *The Lemonade War* way past my bedtime. I just had to find out what happened between Evan and his sister Jesse. I predict that lots of you will want to add this book to your 'must read' list. I'll begin with the characters. Evan seems like a good kid, but he's angry at his little sister, Jesse, and it's our job to figure out why. Jesse seems more complicated than Evan. She's good at understanding math, but struggles to understand people, especially her brother. Things go from bad to worse when they make a bet to see who can raise the most money selling lemonade during the summer. One of the coolest things is that as you read about the kids' lemonade war, you're also learning how to run a business, like the importance of location or how to calculate profit. As the final day of summer approaches, Evan and Jesse will stop at nothing to win. No spoilers here, but I will say that there's stealing and sabotage."

Over time, your students can start giving their own book buzzes to generate excitement around favorite books. Usually teachers set aside a special time—say, half an hour at the end of a Friday or lunchtime—and they invite kids to give book buzzes. Part of being a "reader" is having an identity as a reader. When a child has an opportunity to hold court on a favorite book or author or line of books, that can go a long way toward helping that child develop the identity (and the reputation) of being an avid reader. When kids give their own book buzzes, that will definitely amp up the book culture in your classroom.

Getting Books into Your Students' Hands— and Keeping Track of Books

Of course, your Classroom Library exists to give kids access to books, and it will be important for you to think through that process. If you tell your students that good readers always have a short stack of "books by the bed," you can channel them to select several books to read whenever they go to the classroom library. The number—whether two or eight, for example—will vary depending on the child's reading level, as kids can read briefer and easier books quickly. Children reading books such as Henry and Mudge (level J books), for instance, will probably finish such a book in ten or fifteen minutes, which means that two or three books would barely sustain that child's independent reading period. Because of this, we recommend that students reading below level L fill their baggies with eight to ten books, and then read and reread those titles during the week, building their fluency and deepening their comprehension.

The important thing will be that during independent reading time, students keep a small stack of books at their side, and this stack sustains each reader for at least that day, if not that week. This way, readers can finish one book and shift to the next without missing a step, which supports their reading volume. By decreasing the number of visits to the classroom library, readers gain more time for reading. Then too, when you pull alongside a child, if she has a small collection of books in her baggie, it will be more likely that you'll talk not only about her current book, but also about her reading work over time.

Systems will help keep your books organized, highlight the variety of texts available, help students make smart choices independently, and keep track of books.

Once you introduce children to their Classroom Library, you'll want to recruit them to help institute systems for taking care of the library. One good thing about libraries that are full of raggedy, unwanted, leftover books—no one has to worry about those books walking out the door! But with a drop-dead, beautiful classroom library, full of books that kids will yearn to read, it becomes important to develop systems for using that library well. Those systems will help keep your books organized, highlight the variety of texts available, help students make smart choices independently, and keep track of books.

So the question is: How do kids move books from the classroom library to their bookshelf or baggie? When and how does that happen? Many teachers have an open checkout and return policy running on the honor system. When kids have read all the books in their baggies, they return them to their proper homes in the library. Then readers choose the books they want to read next and stick them into their baggies.

In some classrooms, kids check out and return books whenever they need more books, and in other classrooms, kids visit the library on their allocated day. Many teachers set up a system so that kids sign out each book from the classroom library, using a checkout binder that contains spots for readers to record their names, dates, and the book's title. When a child returns a book, he indicates that in the binder. Such a system can help keep track of books, but you will want to have kids speed through this process so they don't waste precious moments away from reading.

Some teachers use an electronic check-in and checkout system, such as the Booksource Classroom Organizer app. These systems require upfront setup time for the teacher, plus maintenance when new books are added to the library, but they are easy for students to use. (If you have ordered a complete grade-level TCRWP Classroom Library, you will receive details on accessing online resources to accompany the collection, which will include management and sorting data such as book titles, levels, topics, and the like, to help you and your students recreate and keep track of your library resources through many configurations.)

Some teachers invite students to help personalize the classroom checkout system. In the first few days of school, they give students a few half-sheets of white card stock and invite them to create their own library checkout markers. Kids illustrate the checkout markers with their names, along with scenes, titles, and lines from favorite books. Teachers laminate these cards so they'll last. Then, they teach kids that whenever they check out a book from the library, they must leave one of their checkout markers in that book's bin. Once a student runs out of markers, they've reached their limit for checking out books. To return the books to the library, students put a book back for each checkout marker.

In some classrooms, "librarian" is a job, like lunch monitor or line leader. The librarian is responsible for recording how many books classmates checked out at the beginning of the week and how many they returned at the end of the week, perhaps using a clipboard with a list of students' names. Other classrooms use a library pocket system, using a poster board with a library pocket with each reader's name. As part of book shopping, a student jots the books selected for the week on an index card and puts that card in his or her pocket. Teachers can see students' selections at a glance.

Truth be told, however, most of the teachers we researched about systems for checking in/out said, "We have no system." We were shocked! Didn't they lose tons of books each year? The resounding response was no—everyone knows that the library is the most valuable resource of the classroom. Everyone feels responsible for taking care of the library, including returning books.

Above all, the message we are conveying is that there is no one ideal system to manage the flow of books in your classroom. It is important for you and your students to devote time to creating a system and to maintain what you set into motion. You'll convey through your diligence that your classroom library is an enduring resource that gives kids—this year and beyond—access to incredible books. The entire community needs to rally around the job of caring for the library.

Although caring for the library needs to be a shared responsibility, you will probably want a few children to be given the special role of being class librarians. These youngsters can spend time each week reshelving books that have been placed in an "I'm Lost!" or "I Need a Home" bin. A student can also watch over a "Book Hospital" bin, noting if a book has been placed there. Any book that has been torn or damaged needs to be repaired quickly and returned to circulation.

How Can I Keep Interest in the Classroom Library High All Year?

To inspire readers' continued interest in their classroom library, you'll probably want to change your book displays fairly often. At the start of the year, you may display favorites from the prior grade level, surrounding them with related books. In a fifth-grade classroom, the cover of *Because of Winn-Dixie* could be prominently displayed, with a sign saying, "If you loved *Because of Winn-Dixie*, you'll love . . ." and then display several appropriate books.

As the year unfolds, the book bins and the books you place face-out will alter according to your unit of study in language arts and across disciplines. At different times, you may feature character books, historical fiction, or books about magnets or other countries. When you group books together, you encourage kids to read more deeply and to develop in-depth interests.

Over time, your library will come to reflect your students, their identities, interests, and passions. If kids are into skateboarding, make a bin about everything to do with skateboards: ramps, safety, X Games. When you notice that copies of Ron Roy's A to Z Mysteries series are flying off the shelves, gather a bin of similar titles and label it "Cousins to A to Z Mystery Books." When kids come back buzzing after a trip to the art museum, you might send a few of them to the school library and with the librarian's help, fill a basket with artist biographies, titling the basket, "The People behind the Paintings." You may also decide to keep a rotating bin of "Prequels and Sequels to the Read-Aloud Book," alternating titles when a new read-aloud begins. Those evolving book bins keep interest in the library high and allow you to advertise books that youngsters might otherwise miss.

Interestingly, we learned the importance of ways to keep libraries fresh from the Teachers College's Center for Infants and Toddlers. The professor who leads that center once explained to us that you can tell the quality of a preschool by the emphasis it places on storage.

"On storage?" we asked, amazed. Annette explained that the wrong thing to do with young kids is to put all the toys out in the room at the same time, keeping it all out for the year, making the room feel like a giant toy box. For the first week, kids will be on overload, playing for five minutes with one toy, then the next, then the next. Within two weeks, they will have raced through all the surface-level fun activities that the toys suggest, and they'll feel bored. How much better to strategically release a few at a time, choosing ones that combine in a variety of ways: a slide, a truck, a few blocks (imaginary trucks), a cloth, a few stuffed animals. Just that handful of items can inspire lots of thoughtful play.

Similarly, you will want to save some of the really fascinating books in your library for later, knowing that they can launch a new line of work. When one of

those books is brought forward, it can be prominently displayed and you can read bits aloud. Then each book will have a chance to work its magic.

If you are teaching from Units of Study for Teaching Reading (Heinemann 2015), another way to keep interest high in your classroom library is to look ahead to the reading units you'll teach later. If your class will be entering a mystery reading unit in a month or two, you might tuck some of the mystery book bins away until then, unveiling them at the start of the unit as a way to breathe new excitement into the library—as well as to support teaching and learning of that unit. Of course, you won't want to drastically limit the number of titles students have access to, so you'll need to make careful decisions about what books to include and leave out.

Finally, the TCRWP Classroom Libraries have been carefully structured to allow you to add books, filling out and extending the existing structure, whether it's by adding to an existing subcategory, adding a new category or shelf, or adding a new bin label, like "If you liked *Wonder*, you will like . . ." Ask your students for their ideas for new categories and books. This will help to continue to grow kids' enthusiasm for the library.

Tools for the TCRWP Classroom Libraries

Witty, Wise, and Whimsical Tools

Presentation matters. Throw a daisy into a kid's drinking cup, or stick it between the soap and the dishwashing fluid alongside your kitchen sink and that flower looks like No Big Deal. Place the same flower in a tiny vase, set it at the center of your table, perhaps with a bit of white lace under the vase, and you're well on the way toward re-creating the Metropolitan Museum of Art.

Presentation matters for readers, too. When studying classroom libraries prior to launching this endeavor, we were stunned to see how many enthralling books were overlooked simply because they were jammed into bins titled simply "Nonfiction" or "Science."

But of course libraries must not only be appealing places, they must also be accessible.

You'll find that with your complete grade-level library, we've included tools and resources to help get you and your students started creating engaging and inviting instructional and organizational materials.

Book Bin Label Cards: Categorizing Books in Intriguing Ways

Visit any bookstore and watch customers—readers—for just a few minutes. It will immediately be apparent to you the importance of categorizing books, putting them into shelves and baskets that are labeled in quirky or provocative ways to entice readers. Think of the millions of dollars this nation has spent trying to motivate kids to read—and all that was needed (well, not all, but a good start) was for the books to be categorized in intriguing ways. Imagine, for example, a basket titled, "Cool Careers" containing books about spies, clowns, and archeologists. What wonderful conversations readers will have about the jobs they might have in the future!

The TCRWP counts itself lucky to have on its staff talented illustrators, who have made a starter set of bin labels that may help you: "Animal Adaptations," "Sleuths and Snoops", "Class Picks." Each heavy card-stock label has an image that brings a sense of playfulness to the library. If kids like a book in a basket labeled "Misunderstood," they'll probably read the whole basket. By choosing to read a whole *basket* of books, instead of just one book, kids will not only get more reading done, they'll also do more cross-text thinking.

When kids expect a book to be related to other books, they make more intertextual connections, and often the connections are insightful. When readers expect that there must be similarities in character, or theme, or plot, they see similarities that they otherwise wouldn't. It would be an interesting experiment to choose a random book and put it in the "Misunderstood" or the "Unlikely Friendships" basket, and see what insights kids come to. "This *is* an unlikely friendship," they might say of Harry and Hermione, and then have an interesting conversation about that, not realizing the book was misplaced from a "Fantasy" basket!

While we've organized some of the baskets for you by providing bin labels to help group your classroom library into mini-shelves, the suggested groupings are just a starting point. You'll want to do a lot of this work as an ongoing project with your kids. They'll come up with quirky shelves (and new bin labels) that will make you laugh—and will make other kids reach for those books. We've seen kids come up with ideas like "Sports Books for Wimps" and "Brainy Mysteries for Secret Geeks." All sorts of wry, witty, wise, and whimsical mini-shelves come into being when you invite kids to be curators of their library.

Once readers have learned to select books that are within reach for them, you probably won't want your baskets to be titled with levels only. Your youngsters will be glad to select books from baskets labeled "Kids in Charge," stuffed with books like *The Stories Julian Tells* and *Flat Stanley* and *Judy Moody*.

Book Level Labels: Offering Accessibility

You may want to create leveled book bins, perhaps at the beginning of the school year, for some books. (We discuss leveling in much greater detail in Chapter 5.) Should you choose to go this route, you will want to label each individual book with its level so that students can easily rehome books as needed. We have provided miniature level labels to match the illustrated bin cards for this very purpose. Reshelving of books then becomes a job that students can take on as part of their book shopping routines or you might specifically assign a team of "classroom librarians" or "bibliographers" to head up this aspect of library maintenance.

Other teachers may choose not to share lettered reading levels with students, but might color code books by text complexity to make just-right texts accessible, but allow kids to expand their reading lives beyond the confines of level. In this case, you will also want to label your books, but instead of affixing the letter *I* to cover, you might choose to label levels *I* through *K* with the color blue and have readers across this text band select books from within that color label.

At times you will want to mix up books across different levels. You might, for example, put together a range of autumn-themed texts for your readers to peruse in the month of October or collect books about sea creatures as your class prepares for a field trip to the aquarium. In this case, having students be able to identify books that will be accessible is key to their success. Having level or color-coded stickers will make this an easy proposition and will help students quickly predict if a certain book might be too hard, too easy, or just right.

Book Management Data

Included with each shelf of books is a title-by-title list, including topic and level for each book. For those who have chosen a full grade-level Classroom Library, complete library lists are also provided in the online resources, to assist with managing, tracking, and stickering your books. (A separate card is provided in the grade-level Classroom Libraries Tools and Resources box, which provides detailed online resource registration information and instructions.)

Student Sticky-Note Pads: Supporting a
Variety of Reading Strategies

You will also see that we've given you a collection of Post-it note pads that students can use with their books as they read and think. Our goal has been to create notes that say something that great readers often think as they read: "I did *not* see this coming!" or "Stereotype alert!" or "Windows to the character" When kids use these stickies while they read, you'll see that they tend to read more alertly. These Post-its, then, act as lenses to support close, active reading.

Some of these reviewer notes will make you laugh—we laughed at "Grosser than gross!" while imagining exactly which children we know would love using that sticky. When your students use these notes as they read, you'll do more than laugh. Just as you see more in the forest if you know about kinds of trees and can note a pine, an oak, a maple, so, too, kids will see more in a book if they bring lenses such as these to their reading.

We expect that usually, readers will Post-it pages as a "quick jot" to flag favorites and call out "must-reads" for others, or most importantly, as a way to remind themselves to return to those pages during their partner conversation—to support their thinking, talking, and writing about the book. Readers may also decide to leave some of the stickies in a book as tips for future readers. Imagine future

> *When kids use these stickies as lenses, they read more alertly.*

readers encountering a "Watch Out! There are a few tough words on this page" alert. Picture a reader pausing at the end of a book to decide where to insert a few key reviews for future readers, perhaps going back and putting a "Breaking Stereotypes" at the beginning of a chapter they just read. Picture another reader asking herself which pages merit the designation "Life Lesson Learned Here!"

In one of our fifth-grade classrooms, it sounded like this: "Today, you'll each be starting to read a fantasy novel. In any of these novels, you'll want to look for signs of a universal theme—and if you see that in your novel, mark it with a Post-it for the rest of us. You can also look for symbolism and again, if you see it, mark it. You have different stickies for each."

It was beautiful to see kids read with extra alertness, jotting details, noticing things they wouldn't have noticed otherwise. Almost immediately, kids began to suggest other reviews that they believed deserved to be out in the world. "We need one that says 'He's taking her power!'" one reader said. Another asked for "reluctant hero" Soon the class was making many of its own sticky notes—as well as reading with new lenses.

Chapter 4

What's in the TCRWP Classroom Libraries?

Curating the Classroom Libraries

Our goal has been to create classroom libraries that are both high quality and high interest—and we haven't taken this goal lightly. We use the term *curating* because we have aimed to do the kind of work that curators do at the Metropolitan Museum of Art, applying criteria for quality and focus, and making informed decisions about what to include.

The truth is, the kind of readers that you grow will match the libraries that you build. If you want the young people in your care to grow up, accustomed to discovering an author and then reading more books by that writer, then your libraries need to make that likely. If you want young people to fall in love with characters, rooting for them, learning from them, weeping when they are hurt, your libraries need to make that happen. If you want young people to grow up, expecting to experiment with new kinds of stories, the books you put before your children can teach that. So, too, your libraries can teach children that the world is endlessly fascinating, that issues are complex and can be argued from different perspectives, that lessons from history apply to today. The next generation can grow up, delighting in good writing and taking pleasure in language and humor, as well as exciting plots. They can expect that combinations of books spark ideas. The challenge is to nourish our children with books that will make them into the readers, writers, and citizens that we long for them to become.

To achieve the desired balance of high interest and quality, we had extensive conversations with experts in children's literature and literacy. Expert reviewers and critics were part of every decision we made. For each book, we considered if the book would lure a reader to read, and if it would be rewarding when read. Our team included people who know a lot about children's literature, a lot about developmental stages of readers, and a lot about teaching reading successfully.

That means we also asked experts (including ourselves), "Will this book help kids develop skills as powerful readers?" For example, when we and our teams of outside reviewers evaluated books, we used a review sheet ranking the extent to which a particular nonfiction book supported students in "sustained reading to learn." Meanwhile, when reviewing fiction, we ranked books based on whether they supported readers in "rich interpretation, craft, and character work."

As part of our curating process for the Classroom Libraries, we also brought books home to our own kids and our friends' kids, and asked, "Would you look at these books and tell me which you want to read?" We sat in classrooms, asking readers, "Which books in this classroom will get other kids to love reading as much as you do?" Our fingers couldn't type fast enough to capture all their suggestions!

Looking back at our process, it would have been easy to sacrifice quality for immediate interest—after all, we could easily have chosen books that revolve around today's hottest movies, video games, and TV characters, or included sensationalized teenage crime books with lurid covers. But we have held carefully to a joint mission—high interest *and* high quality.

We regard the effort to supply books for kids reading dramatically below benchmark as some of our most important work.

A brief word on below-benchmark libraries. We regarded the effort to supply books for kids reading dramatically below benchmark as our most important work. We could not have worked harder to pull this off. You can be sure that the below-benchmark fifth-grade library is a far cry different from the third-grade benchmark library! We kept the age level of the readers foremost in our minds, and worked hard to choose books that would be both enticing and accessible for those readers. Curating these shelves required exponentially more time than other aspects of this endeavor. We are not entirely content with the results—in some instances, we came from this effort saying, "The books we want simply don't exist yet." We do know, however, that we couldn't have worked harder on this mission, that what we have included in these shelves are the best titles available, and that we'll continue our search.

A word, also, about the nonfiction expository books. We have come to believe that learning to determine importance as kids read nonfiction books (many of which are dense with information) is a critical skill with which most students struggle. Nonfiction often pelts readers with a barrage of little facts, and no one can possible learn those facts quickly enough. We've come to believe that when kids read nonfiction, we need to help them use the text structure to cue them into making a mental outline of the most important aspects of the text. For that reason, we aimed for a large percentage of our nonfiction texts, especially those in levels M–R (levels geared toward strong second-grade readers through mid-range fourth-grade readers), to contain clear, supportive text structures. We were glad to find books with a table of contents, headings, and subheadings. We were glad to find books that gave clear cues indicating, "This is a compare-and-contrast section. Be prepared to notice ways these two subtopics are similar and ways they are different." Of course, we looked for nonfiction texts organized into other text structures as well.

You'll see that while there are some picture books in the collection, most of the books are chapter books. That choice reflects both cost (a picture book often costs as much as three chapter books), and a belief that kids need to do a huge volume of reading. The most cost-efficient way to keep readers who are working with texts that are level M and above "in books" is to supply them with lots and lots of chapter books.

In every part of the TCRWP Classroom Libraries, we considered issues of representation and diversity. We know that all children long for and deserve to see themselves represented in the books in their classroom. We also know that a single book can unwittingly make a stereotype of an identity, or seem a token inclusion. We strove, therefore, with advice from as many experts as possible, to provide texts that celebrate multiple perspectives, cultures, histories, and identities.

We built the Classroom Libraries by curating shelves, most of which had a team of people who worked with a lead curator to evaluate and narrow down the selection of recommended books. The grade 3–5 libraries that resulted from our curating efforts are organized into core shelves, based on grade level, genres, and benchmark/below-benchmark groupings. The core Classroom Libraries for grade 3, for example, contain shelves of high-interest fiction and nonfiction books, mysteries, picture books, biographies, animal books, and poetry books. To add to your own classroom library, or gradually build your collections, each of these shelves can be purchased separately.

The TCRWP Classroom Library collection offers additional shelves that are outside the core library and comprise completely different books from those in the grade-level libraries. For example, we created shelves for teachers who want their students to read within book clubs (also called literature circles) for portions of the school year. Specifically, there are four copies of four or more books for each club, and these club sets are offered for character, historical fiction, fantasy, and interpretation book clubs. You'll find that the books chosen for a club are roughly similar in their level of text complexity so that a club of matched readers will be able to read the books allocated for that club. You'll also see that the choice of books for a club supports interesting cross-textual work.

In addition to book clubs, these libraries provide nonfiction shelves that are based on topics such as geography and world cultures, civil rights, and extreme weather and natural disasters. All of these shelves are designed to help your students develop the habits of purposeful book choice, high reading volume, and thinking across texts.

Curating Specific Shelves

The entire staff of the Teachers College Reading and Writing Project worked shoulder to shoulder to gather recommendations and to review, level, and organize thousands of books into the categories that we imagined would become shelves. Know that for each book that was included, we mulled over a score of other strongly recommended books and eventually set them aside. Always, we have been mindful that the books we put into the hands of young people *matter*.

Before selecting from candidate books for inclusion in any collection or shelf, we made tentative plans for the numbers of books to include in each collection or shelf (that is, the number of mysteries, the number of biographies, and so on) and for the distribution of books at different levels of text complexity that we thought would be important within each of those shelves. For every grade level, we have data on kids' reading levels and the levels of text complexity at which tens of thousands of kids are reading. We used that data to help decide how many books at each level of text complexity were needed for classrooms reading roughly at benchmark levels, and also for classrooms in which kids are reading well below benchmark levels.

For example, for a grade 4 benchmark library (intended for a teacher whose students are mostly reading at grade level, with some below and some above grade level), research in reading levels suggests a plan like this:

Grade 4 Benchmark Library

Levels	Percentage
Levels M/N (benchmark for beginning of 3rd grade)	15%
Levels O/P (benchmark for middle to end of 3rd grade)	20%
Levels Q/R/S (benchmark for the beginning, middle, and end of 4th grade)	45%
Levels T/U (benchmark for beginning and middle of 5th grade)	20%
High-Interest Fiction	**Number of Books**
High-interest fiction of various genres	180
Fantasy	100
Mystery	30
Historical fiction	50
High-Interest Nonfiction	**Number of Books**
High-interest nonfiction	100
Biographies	50
Animals	60
Poetry anthologies	10
Picture books (both fiction and nonfiction)	20

Please see Chapter 5, "Leveling Books, Assessing Students, and Matching Readers to Books," for a detailed discussion of the leveling considerations we brought to the TCRWP Classroom Libraries.

Fiction Shelves

High-Interest Fiction

Curated by Norah Mallaney (Grade 3) and
Alexandra Marron (Grades 4–5)

We intentionally named this shelf, which includes books of many different genres, from realistic fiction, to action-adventure, to sports, "High-Interest Fiction." This collection will be the bulk of your library, and it will introduce students to different authors, genres, and storylines. Some will be favorites your students already know. You'll see books by Judy Blume, Jon Scieszka, and Katherine Paterson. Some will be fresh from the publisher, eagerly read and evaluated for inclusion.

To organize these books, we suggest you begin with some of the bin labels we've included with this Classroom Library, labels like: "LOL," "If You Liked _____, you'll love _____," and "Heartbreak Ahead." For example, for "LOL," some fourth-grade titles (benchmark) might include *Leroy Ninker Saddles Up*, the *Gooney Bird* books, and *Big Nate: Great Minds Think Alike*. We have suggested a small set of books for each of these and many other categories. For additional information on bin labels and other tools, see "Tools for the TCRWP Classroom Libraries" in the "Setting Up, Introducing, and Managing Your Classroom Library" chapter. Your kids will have fun putting books other than the ones we suggest into each of these baskets, and clustering these books will help readers find surprising connections and interests.

Putting books together can also be a more serious endeavor. You want to make it easy for kids to choose books wisely and to move up levels of complexity within types of books they love. The child who loves *Ricky Ricotta and His Mighty Robot* will be delighted to move to *Captain Underpants*, and still later to *Diary of a Wimpy Kid*.

One kind of through-line you will discover will be genre, such as action-adventure, graphic novels, or sports stories. Another type of through-line will be kinds of characters. If your kids love stories about strong girls, it will be a fascinating journey with *Felita, Because of Winn Dixie*, and the like. For each kind of book in this collection, the Classroom Library provides a pathway to other books. Challenge your children to discover these pathways and to create new ones.

The graphic novels in this collection will stun you. (See the next section for more information.) Take one home and read it, if this genre is new to you. The complexity of plot, the seriousness of the themes, and the profound lessons that characters learn in novels like *Roller Girl* and *El Deafo* liken these books to some of the picture books contained in these classroom libraries. The graphic novels, like the picture books, are often richly metaphorical. When your readers dive into these books, you'll see what we've seen. Graphic novels help children become sustained readers. There is picture support for the complexity, and yet the pictures also add intricate, fascinating details, so that it becomes worth it to reread. These books build powerful reading habits.

In the below-benchmark high-interest fiction collection, you'll find books that are immediately engaging. The cover and title spark interest. The books were carefully chosen to *not* be childish. Your readers who are reading books that are geared to readers below your level will need books in which they can develop higher-level thinking skills.

That doesn't mean we shied away from books that are simply funny; *Kung-Pow Chicken* has children laughing out loud. But more important for us, it has them reaching for the next book in the series.

There is a wide range of levels in the fiction shelves, reflecting the knowledge that readers need choice and practice at each level to be able to move on. We want the work they do to be exciting and enveloping. We imagine a reader lying on her belly on the carpet, immersed in *Flora and Ulysses* by Kate DiCamillo, reading entirely for story's sake, not realizing she's practicing skills that will lead her to higher levels of text complexity. Reading progress should not be a race. Readers, especially upper elementary readers, should be living in their levels, exploring the stories within each level and growing the higher-level skills of interpretation, analyzing perspective, and growing ideas.

The books in this collection should support a wide range of readers, as they learn to love books, love reading, and to grow, grow, grow.

Graphic Novels throughout the Libraries

Curated by Eric Hand

Some of you are already fans of graphic novels, and for others, these books will make you a fan. Try reading books like *Hereville: How Mirka Got Her Sword*, and you'll be whisked into the life of a young, strong-willed Orthodox Jewish girl. Graphic novels matter because they engage kids, quickly and deeply. Graphic novels disappear from library shelves as soon as they are placed there. They are also gateway books: hook kids on graphic novels, and kids will find their way to fantasy series. They offer multiple entry points to readers, while presenting complex narratives. Graphic novels matter also because they are gorgeous. It's like having a series of films on your classroom library shelves, only the reader controls the pace, so that he or she has a kind of director's cut, and they can watch and rewatch these thrilling stories at will.

In the Classroom Libraries, graphic novels do not make up a shelf in and of themselves, like mystery or historical fiction. Instead, you'll find graphic novels across the shelves. Most of them are in fantasy and high-interest fiction, and some of them live, as well, in biography or fantasy. As you begin to be more alert to graphic novels, you'll see in bookstores how many great historical-fiction books, adaptations of classics, and nonfiction narratives there are in graphic form. Here, we distribute the graphic novels across the shelves, to entice more readers.

The graphic novels chosen for the libraries have a few qualities that make them fantastic. First, the story has to be engaging and keep kids reading. In fact, we've found that graphic novels help build reading stamina. Never underestimate the power of a great plot. The characters are also complex, allowing students to practice character analysis and interpretation. These books would be effective for your work with students in character studies, in thematic studies, or in any kind of

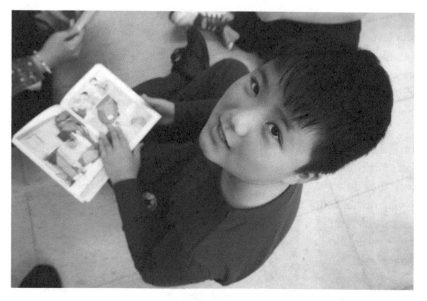

book club. Open up *Bone,* and you'll see that these books are highly metaphoric, with characters who are layered and changeable, and settings that are, frankly, mesmerizing. A lot of these graphic novels also take up serious social issues.

Because graphic novels are about more than words, the art in the books we chose is extraordinary, in terms of arresting visuals and enriching narratives. Students can learn to attend to the important details of visuals, as well as in text. These visuals will help alert students to the mood changes of characters, changes in the setting, and to cueing systems for shifts in time or tone. Often color is used to alert the reader to a flashback or to a dramatic change.

If you are new to reading graphic novels, spend some time in a few of them. Look for how the words and illustrations live within a common space. Unlike picture books, the art in graphic novels is sequential within a page and, therefore, carries a large burden of the storytelling. When panel layout is strong, the movement of the story is intuitive. Your eye naturally flows from left to right and top to bottom, without any confusion as to where to go next. Speech bubbles are stacked to help you follow the flow of conversation. If you read manga, you'll find a kind of "how-to" set of directions on the inside cover (the right cover, of course).

There is one more interesting factor that we've learned from kids reading graphic novels closely. It teaches them to also read challenging nonfiction more closely—the kind of nonfiction where the visuals add significant details and contribute meaning. Simply put, graphic novel readers become more proficient at synthesis.

Fantasy (Grades 4 and 5)

Curated by Lucy Calkins, Katie Clements, Eric Hand, and TCRWP Classroom Library Project Leaders

Fantasy books can be found in two parts of these Classroom Libraries. There are about one hundred fantasy fiction books each in the fourth- and fifth-grade libraries (both benchmark and below-benchmark), and there are also separate Fantasy Book Club Shelves, containing four copies each of sixteen books. (Fantasy Book Club is described in more detail in the book club section that follows.)

That's a lot of fantasy—but we know there is nothing better at turning kids into readers for life than fantasy. Fantasy books, especially fantasy series, set kids up to read with tremendous volume and increased complexity. Think of Harry Potter. More than 450 million copies of Harry Potter books have been sold worldwide, the best-selling book series since records have been kept.

What draws children to Harry Potter will also draw them to Dragon Slayers' Academy and Sisters Grimm. Fantasy lets children escape from the ordinary troubles of their lives. Whether they live in that world within the pages of a single book, or they inhabit it over a series such as Narnia, children long for the fantastic settings and wild adventures of these worlds.

In the fantasy portion of the library, we chose books that will boost your students' volume of reading, and their ability to deal with complexity. To increase volume, we introduced the most engaging fantasy series by including the first few books of each series. Rather than including the entire series, we wanted to introduce as many authors and series to your children as possible. Expect to help your avid readers find the rest of these series, and keep these books in mind for future book orders or fairs!

Thinking about complexity, we included many fantasy books that allow students to study complicated settings, to trace multiple plot lines and multiple themes, and to investigate characters who are archetypes and characters who are not always what they seem. These novels are also rife with social issues. By the end of book one of the Dragon Slayers' Academy series, for instance, the main character has become a celebrated slayer of dragons who secretly wants to befriend dragons, his sidekick is a boy who realizes his struggle is more with overeating than with defeating fiery creatures, and the best male warrior in the school turns out to be a girl who is cross-dressing. Know that these novels will be great for character studies, for social issues book clubs, and for any interpretation work, as well as for studies of the genre.

Fantasy novels will be great for character studies, book clubs, and interpretation work.

In the below-benchmark shelves, there are, more often, the first few books of series, or in rare instances, the whole series. Including more of a series will help your below-grade-level readers choose multiple books at a time, read fast and furious without interruption, and begin to synthesize across hundreds of pages. In this way, reading the fantasy series in your library equips kids to tackle longer, denser, more complicated books in the future.

Mystery

Curated by Brooke Geller and Alissa Reicherter

Ask a room full of adult readers to name their favorite children's books, and you're bound to hear mystery series such as Nancy Drew or Hardy Boys. Or ask a room full of adults what they read, and at least half will tell you that a lot of their books are mysteries. If you have a hard time luring your students to read, offer a pile of mysteries and that resistance often melts away.

Mysteries are an exciting, fast-paced, action-packed genre. Readers are hooked from the start, drawn in by the plot and the chance to race alongside the detective as he or she solves the mystery. In some ways, mysteries are like starter kits to the more complex and complicated fiction reading to come. Unlike a lot of adult mysteries, in the mysteries that many third- and fourth-graders read, the characters are often less complex than those in other genres, and the problems they encounter tend to be in-your-face, easy for the alert reader to spot. These books make it worthwhile to pay close attention to detail.

Mystery books will give children a chance to learn and practice important reading skills such as envisioning, predicting, monitoring for sense, retelling, summarizing, and synthesizing. Mystery readers also have to keep track of multiple suspects, which gives children an opportunity to think about secondary characters, not just the main character. This helps students prepare to read more challenging fiction with richer characters, plots, and themes later on.

In the Mystery shelves in these Classroom Libraries, you'll find many series, and this is especially true in the libraries that contain books written at lower levels. In lower levels, there are beloved series like Cam Jansen, Nate the Great, Bones, and The High-Rise Private Eyes. These are classics for a third-grade classroom library. The reliable, predictable nature of these series allows readers to get lost in suspenseful plots and practice the alert, edge-of-your-seat reading that we want children to know and do. Also, as kids read book after book in a series, they come to know the characters well and can do stronger predicting work. They come to know that when Cam says, "Click!" or Nate gets a hankering for some pancakes, solutions are just around the corner!

The fourth- and fifth-grade libraries contain series such as Sammy Keyes and Scream Street, but they also contain more stand-alone titles, some of which contain elements of suspense. You'll see titles like Ellen Raskin's *The Westing Game* and Andrew Clements's *Room One: A Mystery or Two*. Graphic novels are introduced in the fourth-grade collection, such as the Hardy Boys graphic novel series. David Sobol's *Two-Minute Mysteries* are in the fifth-grade library.

In the below-benchmark shelves, you'll find texts that are easy to grasp and also honor your readers' maturity levels, such as The Clubhouse Mysteries series, which is both lower level and age-appropriate. You'll notice lots of series to hook readers and keep them reading across multiple books as well as engaging titles and covers to help grab readers' interest right from the start.

Among the books with picture support, the graphic novels, and the longer, print-dense stories, you should find mysteries for all your readers. Expect to see your students huddled over the pages, unwilling to put the books down when the time for reading ends. Mysteries launch children into being readers who stay up late, flashlight in hand, desperate to find out "whodunit." We've aimed to ensure this selection of titles does just that!

Historical Fiction

Curated by Shana Frazin and Simone Fraser

Historical fiction books can be found in two parts of these libraries. There are individual copies of historical fiction books in the fourth- and fifth-grade libraries (both benchmark and below-benchmark), and there are also separate Historical

Fiction Book Club Shelves, each containing four copies of four titles, described in the book club section that follows.

Historical fiction is an important genre because it provides readers with both a buckle-your-seatbelt plot line and an inspirational life lesson. These books tell stories of times of crisis throughout history, weaving in stories about how a person—usually a young person—finds a way to rise to the challenges of his or her times. This is a potent mix. Your youngsters will be moved by these books, making it easy for you to teach them higher-level interpretation skills.

The books in the grades 4 and 5 collections reflect three goals: take kids on a high-energy, exciting ride; thoughtfully and appropriately immerse children into a place and time; and highlight the power of one individual, often a child, who makes a difference in the world. For example, we included *New Shoes* by Susan Lynn Meyer, which tells the story of one girl, Ella Mae, tackling issues of segregation. We want reading to help kids get that swelling-in-the-breast feeling that comes when a person begins to think, "Maybe I can make a difference too."

You may need to personally introduce historical fiction books to individual kids. A child's first thought when looking at the cover may be, "This person is going to be nothing like me." Yet when you bring the same book over and say, "I've been thinking about you, and the kind of person you are, and I think the kid in this book is actually a lot like you," your student will feel eager to start reading that book. It only takes one or two "introductions" for reader and historical fiction to become fast friends. It's an important relationship, for historical fiction inherently introduces complexity. The character lives in a place you have not lived, in a time you have not inhabited.

Expect to have maps and historical atlases on hand. There are, of course, many geography resources available both in print and online, but you may find the non-fiction resources in the Geography and World Culture shelves for Grades 3 and 4 especially useful as your readers research the events and places their books are set in. (For more information see the section on Geography and World Cultures Shelves.)

If you can lure your children into historical fiction, they'll become powerful readers, able to handle complexity, skilled at on-the-run research, and empathetic to characters seemingly unlike themselves.

Picture Books

Curated by Lucy Calkins and the Entire TCRWP Staff

Though the number of picture books in this shelf is small, each one is a jewel. Some of these books you'll want to read aloud to your whole class, or to a small group. Expect students to pore over and reread them. That is one of the joys of picture books. They call to mind experiences from our earliest memories of reading. The ones chosen here are also written at

multiple levels, so there are levels of metaphor, meaning, and humor that readers appreciate at different times in their reading lives.

These picture books often take up serious issues of justice and injustice, which is ironic, as they often look as if they are for younger readers. Pick up *The Other Side*, though, and you are introduced to children trying to cross the color line, against the prevailing wisdom of adults. Open *One Green Apple*, and you are suddenly in an apple orchard alongside an immigrant child. Read *Fly Away Home* and you spend your days with young Andrew, who is homeless with his father, living in an airport. As a reader, you realize that some stories and feelings are universal.

Other books introduce characters with complicated internal struggles. *Dancing in the Wings* puts you in the shoes of a girl who is uncomfortable in her too tall body. *Mufaro's Beautiful Daughters* shows two sisters who learn how the kindness inside them can change their lives. *Thank You, Mr. Falker* tells about a girl who can't make sense of letters, and the trust she begins to feel toward a teacher who believes in her.

These beautiful books tackle big issues in the world and big issues for children. They will anchor your classroom library and your children's reading lives, and will also serve as mentor texts for writing. The availability of stories that represent different histories, peoples, cultures, and identities is far greater for picture books than any other genre, so we included as many books as possible that increased representation.

Poetry

Curated by Lucy Calkins and TCRWP Classroom Library Project Leaders
This shelf includes anthologies and chapbooks, or collections of poems by a single author. What unites this poetry is that the language, themes, topics, and content are relevant to kids' lives. Some poems are witty and entertaining; they make you laugh. Some are observant; they help you to look at what's often overlooked. Some are serious; they linger in the spaces of loss and hurt. Naomi Shihab Nye will bring you voices of children who have lost their homelands. Nikki Grimes will have your tongue twisting with her rhythms and joy in language, while you ponder the underlying seriousness of her themes. Shel Silverstein will have you laughing in delight.

> *The poetry shelves will ignite your students' interest in contemporary verse.*

The poetry books in these shelves will be important in three ways. First, you will turn to poetry yourself as a teacher, mining these shelves for poems to teach interpretation, to practice fluency, to set alongside and inside your reading lessons on interpreting characters and themes and figurative language. Every time you use a poem in a reading lesson, it reminds your students of the fascinations of this genre, and you'll see them, later, pulling out some of these poetry books and poring over pages. Notice which students are drawn to poetry, and later you'll recommend the chapter books in the High-Interest Fiction collection written in verse: *Love That Dog, Hate That Cat, Inside Out and Back Again,* and *Out of the Dust.* There are so many funny, witty, serious, gorgeous stories told in verse now for young people. These poetry shelves will ignite your students' interest in contemporary verse.

A second way this collection will be important will be to provide mentor texts for children's own poetry writing. The collection includes poetry whose form and content are appealing to young people. Each writer has a different style; each brings a unique perspective. They all bring playfulness and discipline to their work, so that students can study these poems as mentor texts, inquiring how poets use white space and line breaks; how they develop metaphors; what role repetition, alliteration, and so on play in their poems. This is a great collection for kids who read as writers.

A third way you might turn to this collection is a way that can be overlooked in a classroom that has become too obsessed with standards or benchmarks. There may be moments in your classroom when you see that a child is hurting. Children grow up with pain that may be immense, and they have virtually no control over what happens to them. They can, though, learn that they are not alone. When you see a child who seems solitary or desolate, when you notice sadness in a child, know that poetry brings solace. You could say: "I've been thinking about you. I thought this poem might be meaningful to you. This is for you."

Nonfiction Shelves

High-Interest Nonfiction (with related fiction)

Curated by Kelly Boland Hohne and TCRWP Staff

To create this shelf, we set out to locate, select, and organize eighty to one hundred nonfiction books on science and social studies topics (other than books focused mainly on animals), ensuring that these books were of sufficiently high interest to lure children into engaged reading. To create the shelf, we not only visited classrooms to study their nonfiction collections, we also brought books home to read to our own kids, asking, "Do you love this book? Would you want it to be included in the library?" We searched the shelves of bookstores, looking for gems, and we read and read and read.

Our abiding goal was to curate a collection of high-interest nonfiction books that allowed readers to learn deeply about the world. All too often, students leap for nonfiction books that exclaim an amazing or crazy fact on each page. Reading random, interesting facts isn't the same as reading to learn deeply about one topic. Curating this collection became all about balance— making sure we included a few of those "Did you know this amazing fact?" books for every grade, but also making sure that most books promote deep, sustained reading to learn.

Our goal was to create a collection of high-interest nonfiction books that allowed readers to learn deeply about the world.

That means that after asking, "Will kids be into this topic? Will they find this book fascinating?" we also asked, "How easy is it to learn from this book?" We made sure that when readers bring a knowledge of text structures to their reading, using that knowledge to discern main ideas and key details, they have deep access to the text's content. We also know that as texts get more complex, the structures are bound to become less clear-cut and the headings less supportive (if there are headings at all).

Of course, the thing that drives a reader to work hard on comprehension is a commitment to the content. To say we looked for high-interest books is an understatement. We searched for and found books about mysterious events, black holes, skateboarding, what it's like inside a bakery, weird plants, monster trucks, and the challenges of living in historical time periods.

Once we said "yes" to the books, we began the next important step of the process—creating smaller subcategories within each grade's high-interest nonfiction library. When we asked kids in classrooms to tell us their favorite nonfiction books, many responded by telling us a *topic*, not a book. They said, "I like to read about robots" or "sports" or "sharks." So we knew we would organize these books in topic sets. We also wanted to make these subcategories so tantalizing that a reader couldn't resist reading through the entire basket. So we created a subcategory on "Cool Careers" in third grade, including books like *Backstage Pass: Fashion* and *Sweet: Inside a Bakery* and *A Day in the Life of a Firefighter.* Another subcategory is "How does that work?" with books on how magic tricks, toilets, and other things work. Other subcategories include "Mysterious Events and Creatures," "Disasters," "Discovering the Prehistoric," "How to Survive Anything," "The Military and Espionage," "Robots and Machines" "Places to Explore," and many more. As Steph Harvey recently reminded us, "Ultimately it's the content that's seductive." We believe that these baskets of well-written, informative books will entice readers to be seduced by rich, thought-provoking content and to become more knowledgeable about the world.

As students read within a basket, one hope is that they will start to see broad connections across a subtopic. For instance, if fourth-graders delve into a "Feats of Engineering" basket, they may read across stacks of books, such as *Deserted Stone Cities, Building Greenscrapers*, and *This Bridge Will Not Be Gray.* These readers will begin to form questions about how and why people build, their challenges over time, and how people have overcome those challenges, as well as the effects on civilization.

You will find that within the nonfiction collection, there are a few fiction books that are related to the nonfiction. For example, you'll see *You Are the First Kid on Mars* by Patrick O'Brien alongside related nonfiction.

You'll see that there are many lower-level nonfiction books for the below-benchmark fourth- and fifth-grade libraries that are engaging and do not look as if they were for younger readers. We especially looked for interesting, bizarre topics to try to hook these readers, but also included books on science topics like pollution and recycling because those books allow students to learn about the world around them.

We hope you regard the baskets containing subordinate categories as starter ideas. If you see your students loving a "Cool Careers" basket, that suggests that you might get more books for that basket. We have offered examples of books that could go into these subcategories, but these subcategories are not exhaustive. New and great nonfiction will continue to be published. You can bring books in and ask your students into what subcategory they belong, or ask students to think of a new subcategory.

A library is a flexible, living organism, as Ranganathan argued, and it should grow and evolve. Our best hope is that the nonfiction books chosen for these Classroom Libraries start your children on a journey of curiosity and wonder and learning about the world.

Animals

Curated by Kathleen Tolan and TCRWP Classroom Library Project Leaders

When curating these shelves, our priority was to make sure that we selected books that would tap into children's natural interest in animals and use that interest to empower kids to develop as nonfiction readers.

We know these books will support children's curiosity about and engagement with the world, while supporting their skills as nonfiction readers. It is all too common for students to skim through a book or a pile of books, dipping in here or there to harvest a curious fact, to admire a photograph. We wanted the animals collection to support a deeper, more engaged, and committed sort of reading.

In this world of twenty-first-century literacy, readers don't learn about a topic by reading a single source. Instead, a reader usually reads several texts on a topic, with each text offering different and sometimes conflicting information. Books about animals are organized in a way that supports readers zooming in on a specific section of a book, reading that section, then finding a section of another book that addresses a similar subtopic and reading that, and then synthesizing the information learned from the various sources. For example, three books on gorillas will each contain a chapter on baby gorillas, though in each book, the chapters may be titled differently ("Gorilla Families," "Growing Up," or "Gorilla Life Cycles").

You don't have to be teaching our Units of Study for Teaching Reading to find these libraries useful, but if you are, you'll be pleased to see how the shelf supports kids' research clubs. For example, Units of Study for Teaching Reading contains a unit, *Research Clubs*, which is a favorite third-grade unit. Some fourth- and fifth-grade teachers who teach kids reading well below benchmark teach that third-grade unit to their older readers, since it is a high-interest unit that supports foundational, nonfiction reading skills. Whether you are teaching with support from *Research Clubs* or not, you will probably want to use animal books to help at least your third-graders or your below-benchmark fourth- and fifth-graders read selected chapters from one book, another, another, rather than reading each book, head-to-toe.

You'll see, then, that in both the benchmark and below-benchmark third-grade libraries and in the fourth- and fifth-grade below-benchmark libraries, the collection contains many books that address a particular animal (say, sharks) in ways that will help kids to synthesize information across those texts. The collection of books on a particular animal has been assembled with attention to levels of text complexity, with many books written at similar levels of text complexity, and some at higher levels. Once a reader has read four books about bears, that reader will be able to read a more complex text on that topic.

Of course, once a reader has read several books about each of a few animals, then that reader is also primed to categorize animals ("these are all sea animals") and to set out on the work of comparing and contrasting animals. How are these various sea animals alike? Different? This question will set readers up to reread their texts with a new purpose in mind. Readers are also primed to think about concepts that pertain to many animals (animal adaptations, animal intelligence). In all the fourth- and fifth-grade libraries, including the below-benchmark libraries, we also include many of those books.

When developing the below-benchmark animal shelves, one of our biggest goals was to find books that are not hard to read but are engaging for kids. In an effort to promote the animal books in our below-benchmark libraries, we categorized the books into baskets that we labeled with engaging titles: "Amazing Animal Talents," "Dangerous Animals," "Gross and Bizarre!" Children might begin by using these bin titles as jumping-off points for their thinking work. For instance, what makes each of these animals amazing, dangerous, or gross? Which animal of all those represented in a bin is the most amazing or the grossest? These investigations could carry readers from book to book.

The benchmark libraries for grades 4 and 5 include books that each address a particular animal, but as one moves toward more complex nonfiction texts, the books that are available—and irresistible—change. Readers who are working at and above level R, for example, will find that the library contains fascinating books that are not all about a single animal, but address fascinating animal categories, such as in Seymour Simon's classic, *Animals Nobody Loves*, or in the book basket labeled "Gross and Bizarre!"

Biography

Curated by Cynthia Satterlee and TCRWP Classroom Library Project Leaders

To develop the biography shelves, we considered two overall criteria: Does a book qualify as great literature? And would kids be able to read it and *want* to read it? Our efforts were influenced by our focus on supporting students' skills at reading

narrative nonfiction and by our knowledge that kids need to learn not only *about* but also *through* reading.

Biographies offer a wonderful forum for teaching youngsters strategies for determining importance when reading nonfiction texts. It is mind-boggling to consider how much new information a nine-year-old needs to assimilate when reading a biography about Abe Lincoln, for example. To construct an understanding of Lincoln's life, such a reader would need to glean something about Illinois, the Emancipation Proclamation, debates, Westward Expansion, the Civil War, slavery, the right to vote, and so on.

That nine-year-old attempting to understand Lincoln's life will need help figuring out which information in the text is important and which, less important. To help biography readers determine importance, you will want them to know that biographies are apt to be structured as stories. When reading about Abe Lincoln's life, a reader will want to think about the same things that she thinks about when reading fictional stories. Who is this character? What is he like? What motivates him? What gets in the way? Who are the other most important people in this story and what are they like? What is their relationship with the main subject (in this case, with Lincoln)? Then,

too, readers need to think about what the trouble is that the character faces, and how that character rises to those challenges.

Of course, readers of biographies can also read in such a way that they gather information related to important subtopics. Perhaps above all, a reader of Abe Lincoln's biography focuses on the Emancipation Proclamation, collecting information much as she would have done when reading a straight expository nonfiction text on the topics. Rather than selecting books that readers will fact-mine, dipping in and out of them, we preferred books that we believed kids would actually hunker down and read.

The effort to select biographies that children could read—and to do this for children working at different grade levels and levels of text complexity—sometimes channeled us toward picture books rather than book-length biographies. When this happened, we made a point to choose picture books that contained lots of text. As with all our collections, we generally avoided including more than a few books from any one series, feeling that if students love a series, they could find the remaining volumes at the school or public library. We felt it would be more helpful if we exposed kids to more series and more authors, rather than providing great depth in any one series.

We also included biographies that encourage readers to develop lines of inquiry as they read, going from reading one book to reading another related book. You will see many examples of texts that go together, whether it's a few books on the same person, or a few books on people who have similar jobs or can otherwise be compared and contrasted. Students can note how different authors can describe the same person, event, or activity from varying sides. A fourth-grade library, for example, contains *Barack Obama* by Caroline Crosson Gilpin and *Barack Obama: Son of Promise, Child of Hope* by Nikki Grimes—two books that are just asking to be compared.

Meanwhile, there are also books that help youngsters learn about ways that people have contributed to the world. We included books by and about people from many corners of the world who made a positive difference. In *Wangari's Trees of Peace*, author Jeanette Winter writes about Wangari Maathai, a Kenyan woman who travels home to find that her childhood forest has been cut down. Maathai, the first African woman to earn a PhD in science, decided to plant a few trees. We thought it important for students to read about how something that began as a simple action turned into a widespread grassroots movement, which ultimately earned Maathai a Nobel Peace Prize.

In terms of our curating process, though we began with a towering pile of biographies, we eliminated scores of books early on. By the end, we had relatively few contenders from which to select. Two experts on biography—Anita Silvey, former editor of *The Horn Book Magazine* and author of several biographies, including the award-winning *Untamed: The Wild Life of Jane Goodall*, and Betty Carter, professor emerita of children's and young adult literature at Texas Woman's University and former reading teacher and school librarian—knew almost every book in our huge piles. They pointed out books that couldn't reasonably qualify as a "true biography." Then, too, if a major portion of a character's life was not included in the life story about that character, we tended to disqualify that book. We also deleted outdated books, such as a book on contemporary figures.

We went round and round the question of whether to include fictionalized biography. Some biographies that are popular with kids contain enough fictionalized scenes and invented dialogue that they are probably best called "quasi-biography." We settled on including those that represented the best of a few series that might, at times, cross the line between nonfiction and fiction.

Finally, we always made a great effort to include high-interest biography, like *The Inventors of LEGO Toys*, and *Whoosh! Lonnie Johnson's Super-Soaking Stream of Inventions*.

Third-Grade Far Below-Benchmark Leveled Library Shelf

Curated by TCRWP Classroom Library Project Leaders

Across each Classroom Library and within each shelf, we took seriously the job of finding the best possible books for students reading far below benchmark. One of our biggest revelations about the needs of below-benchmark readers came as we were making decisions for the high-interest fiction collection for the third-grade below-benchmark library. Using student performance data from schools across New York City, we decided the third-grade below benchmark libraries should range mostly between level F and level M to adequately meet the needs of below-grade-level third-grade students.

Our hope was to find books that kids reading at levels F/G could read, written in ways to help them do some of the higher-level comprehension work that their classmates are being taught. For example, third-graders work to understand characters that are complex enough that they may act one way in one setting and another way in another setting. Third-graders are aware that a character might seem very different in one relationship than in another. However, when searching for books written for kids reading at levels F/G, it wasn't easy to find books that do that kind of rich character development. Among books written at level F, for example, we found many books in which the characters aren't complex, nor do they change or grow much. Then too, below level I, we found it hard to locate true adventure books or sports novels or enthralling series books.

By searching high and low and asking hundreds of people for help, we were able to locate many titles that will serve the needs of readers in levels F–I. Still, we know that the titles for this shelf are not all the most thrilling ones in your collection, and we know your below-benchmark readers would rather have *Big Nate* or *Because of Winn Dixie* in their hands. Therefore, we encourage you and your students to look at this shelf as a stepping-stone toward reading longer, more engaging, and complex texts.

This Third-Grade Far Below-Benchmark Leveled Library Shelf is meant to supplement the level F–I books that are already included across the third-grade below-benchmark Classroom Library shelves for fiction and nonfiction. We know that readers at these levels and lower need many books to read to keep up their stamina and grow up to new levels. The Third-Grade Far Below-Benchmark Leveled Library Shelf is a good start, but we recommend this shelf be purchased to bolster the number of books at levels F–I—books that meet the requirements of the level and are engaging even for older readers. This shelf can also supplement and extend levels included in the fourth-, fifth-, or even sixth-grade libraries, if needed for your class.

Additional Shelves

Fairy Tales Shelf (Grade 3)

Curated by TCRWP Classroom Library Project Leaders

Selecting the fairy tales for this shelf was a treat and a delight. Nothing captures kids' imaginations or hearts like fairy tales. Still, as we read through stacks of fairy tales we followed a few guiding principles. First, we wanted this shelf to support a strong foundation in this much-loved genre. This means we included a beautifully written and illustrated anthology of classic fairy tales that contains stories by Hans Christian Andersen, the Brothers Grimm, and Charles Perrault as well as several Caldecott-worthy (because they contain drop-dead gorgeous illustrations) stand-alone classics, such as *Lon Po Po: A Red-Riding Hood Story from China* by Ed Young.

We also wanted this shelf to support narrative writing. We've discovered that students' narrative writing grows by leaps and bounds when they are taught to adapt the classics and write original fairy tales. For those of you using our Units of Study for Teaching Opinion/Argument, Information, and Narrative Writing, this shelf is a perfect companion for the Grade 3 unit *Once Upon a Time: Adapting and Writing Fairy Tales* (Heinemann 2013). In addition to the classics, this shelf contains several adaptations of classics so that your writers can investigate the whys and hows of adapting fairy tales by reading and studying books such as *Cinder Edna* by Ellen Jackson and *Goldilocks and the Three Dinosaurs* by Mo Willems.

Finally, this collection supports deeper comprehension work. When teaching perspective and point of view you might read *The True Story of the Three Little Pigs* by Jon Scieszka. This version retells the classic tale from the perspective of the wolf, inviting readers to question whether the wolf is truly big and bad. Likewise, this collection with its many versions and adaptations of fairy tales is ideal for compare-and-contrast work and for analyzing author's craft. (Why and how did the

author modify the original fairy tale?) Whatever the skill, this collection of highly engaging short text will instruct and inspire.

Geography and World Cultures Shelves (Grades 3 and 4)

Curated by Emily Butler Smith and TCRWP Classroom Library
Project Leaders

Globalization has changed our concept of what it means to be a citizen. Today, we all are much more aware of the larger world—and our kids will need even more awareness of that whole wide world. It was always important for an educated person to know about the geography of the world. After all, the shape and content of our lives is very dependent on geography. But geography is becoming more important than ever in the twenty-first century.

We curated the Geography and World Culture Shelves, guided by the belief that students need to grow up learning about different cultures and perspectives. Being exposed to a diversity of perspectives through books, such as *Far North* (Vanishing Culture Series) and *Only the Mountains Do Not Move: A Masai Story of Culture and Conversation*, will support students in becoming more critical readers and thinkers—and better world citizens.

To help us manage and decide among the vast number of possible books for these shelves, we developed a gridlike plan to help us responsibly "cover" the broad field of geography. We populated each of the shelves with maps, atlases, and books on cartography, and then selected a book or two about each of the seven continents. Then we layered the continent shelves with books that explored life in several different parts of that continent.

You can think of the shelf as an inverted pyramid. At the base of the pyramid are the gateway books, the ones about an extensive physical or cultural region, such as Asia or Africa. From there, we've included books on nations within each continent, books that highlight the human and physical geography within a given place. At the tip of the pyramid are books about the particularities of daily life and how these experiences are the same and different across the world, such as *Coming to America: A Muslim Family's Story*. Together, these text sets encourage readers to compare their lives to the lives of others and to also form understandings of their place in relation to others' around the world.

You'll find the Grade 3 Geography and World Cultures shelf already included in the complete On-Benchmark Grade 3 Classroom Library, and also available separately. For Grade 4, the Geography and World Cultures shelf is separated from the grade-level libraries.

American Revolution Shelf (Grades 4–5)

Curated by Janet Steinberg

In curating the American Revolution Shelf, our goal was to find fifty titles that show multiple perspectives, cover the duration of the war, and allow for rich work to be done in the classroom. We aimed for books that would allow your students to dive into the big topics and subtopics of the revolution (causes, results, people's experiences). At the same time, we wanted these texts to be rich in supporting nonfiction reading work.

You'll notice that the titles cover a range of perspectives and points of view. This is deliberate to help you and your students explore the notion that the study of history is not about learning one story. Rather, it is about exploring multiple accounts of an event and coming up with interpretations that provide insight into past events and current applications. We hope that books like *The Split History of the American Revolution* and *Voices of the American Revolution* help you and your students to do this work.

To support the development of reading skills, we were careful to choose books that reflect a range of nonfiction writing structures and craft moves. This particular shelf has books that illustrate cause and effect, compare and contrast, and chronological retellings of history. We also sought books that had beautiful narrative nonfiction writing that allows for rich character analysis to better understand motivations, struggles, and traits. Finally, you'll see that graphic novels are also included. We are excited that so many graphic novel authors are writing about history, as it invites readers to extend into a different format, and readers who love graphic novels to explore history.

Civil Rights Shelf (Grades 4–5)

Curated by Emily Butler Smith

Similar to the Westward Expansion and American Revolution Shelves, we decided to assemble a shelf devoted to civil rights because it is a topic of study for many schools and a topic of interest for many students. Further, there are an incredible number of books available for upper elementary readers on this topic. We selected more than thirty titles for this shelf. It is important to note that we chose a variety of texts about the broader topic of civil rights, which includes women's suffrage as well as the civil rights movement in the 1960s in the United States.

As with the Government Shelf (see the following description), we chose books on a range of topics and levels so that students could develop a broader awareness of the topic by reading survey books, but could also delve into detail by reading several titles on a subtopic. For example, most fourth- or fifth-graders would benefit from reading a text that is broad in scope, such as *Life in the Time of Rosa Parks and the Civil Rights Movement* by Terri DeGezelle, but may then want to read across several titles about a subtopic like school integration.

We also included a variety of types of texts. In addition to straightforward expository nonfiction, you'll find picture books such as Kadir Nelson's Coretta Scott King Award winner, *Heart and Soul*, Selina Alko's *The Case for Loving*, Pam Muñoz Ryan's *When Marian Sang*, and *Elizabeth Leads the Way* by Tanya Lee Stone and Rebecca Gibbon, as well as several issues of *Cobblestone* magazine, which provide opportunities for cross-text synthesis. In our pilot classrooms, we were thrilled to see kids reading across issues of *Cobblestone* such as *Unsung Heroes of the Civil Rights Movement*. Students dug into longer articles and engaged with some shorter puzzles and cartoons. We're excited to offer this kind of range to the readers in your classrooms, too.

Government Shelf (Grades 4–5)

Curated by Emily Butler Smith

When we began curating these Classroom Libraries, we did not plan to create a shelf on Government, but the books themselves convinced us. As the 22,000 books from recommenders flooded into our review process, we found ourselves stopped in our tracks by books on government. Meanwhile, every day, more turmoil occurs within our own government, and we think and talk often about how necessary it is for the next generation of Americans to grow up with a knowledge of government.

You'll see that titles in this shelf represent a range of subtopics related to government and a range of levels of text complexity. We selected some books because they are well written and succeed in teaching broad and important information. We also wanted this shelf to allow students to become interested in government subtopics and to pursue those interests by reading a pathway of related books. For instance, a student could read *Governments Around the World* by Ernestine

Giesecke to develop a bird's-eye understanding of different governments and to compare and contrast them. Alternatively, the student could read a collection of titles about democracy, such as *Our Democracy* by Ariella Tievsky and *The Democratic Process* by Mark Friedman.

In addition to straightforward expository nonfiction, you'll find this shelf includes picture books like the Caldecott Award winner, *So You Want to Be President?* by Judith St. George and David Small, and *I Pledge Allegiance* by Bill Martin Jr, Michael Sampson, and Chris Raschka. The shelf also contains a few carefully selected issues of *Cobblestone* magazine. As Richard Allington points out in *What Really Matters for Struggling Readers*, adults spend the majority of their time reading newspapers and magazines, so we wanted to provide students with access to magazines because we believe they are frequently more engaging to young readers, too (Allington 2001, 61). We also appreciate the thematic structure of *Cobblestone* issues because of the authentic opportunities for cross-text synthesis provided for readers.

Westward Expansion Shelf (Grades 4–6)

Curated by Emily Butler Smith

The period of Westward Expansion spans roughly one hundred years of United States history. It was an exciting and turbulent time of national growth, tremendous conflict, and cultural exchange—a time period that helped shape the America that you and your students live in today. When curating this shelf, we selected forty-plus texts that are diverse in focus, perspective, level, and format. There are a number of survey books to provide readers with overviews on topics related to this period. You'll also see texts that will help students pursue subtopics, such as the journey of Lewis and Clark, the impact of Westward Expansion on Native American groups, and the rapidly changing technology of the time period.

This shelf was shaped by our thinking as teachers of reading. We selected texts structured with headings and subheadings that can cue students in to organizational patterns of text, such as compare and contrast, cause and effect, and chronology. We also selected narrative nonfiction texts, knowing it would help students to read those texts looking for characters' traits, motivations, struggles, changes, and lessons learned.

But most of all, we know that the texts that will help students read nonfiction with comprehension need to be interesting, sparking students' curiosity. We know that readers of all ages are fascinated by the unknown, and therefore we looked for texts that brought fresh perspectives to this time in history, such as *The Foul, Filthy American Frontier: The Disgusting Details about the Journey Out West* by Heather Schwartz.

It was a priority to include multiple perspectives about this controversial time in American history. You'll see evidence of this in the selection of books like *Buffalo Soldiers: Heroes of the American West* by Brynn Baker, *The Split History of Westward Expansion in the United States* by Nell Musolf, and *Thunder Rolling Down the Mountain: The Story of Chief Joseph and the Nez Perce* by Agnieszka Biskup.

We recognize that history is not inevitable; instead, it is about the choices people have made and continue to make. Through including a variety of perspectives, we can support students' emerging understanding of this guiding principle. Further,

we hope that with increased awareness of multiple perspectives, readers will seek out additional resources to strive for a more nuanced and complex understanding of this time period—and really of any time period.

Finally, we assembled this shelf not only because it is a topic of study in many fourth- and fifth-grade classrooms and because it is of interest across the United States, but also as a resource for teachers who are teaching the Grade 5 unit, *The Lens of History*, part of the Units of Study in Opinion, Information, and Narrative Writing (Heinemann 2012).

Extreme Weather and Natural Disasters Shelves (Grade 4 Below-Benchmark and On-Benchmark)

Curated by Mike Ochs

Why weather? Hurricanes, tornadoes, floods, droughts—these extreme conditions are fascinating to children, just as they are to adults. Watch a video of a tornado and one is bound to ask "why?" and "how?"

To develop these shelves, we considered the broader goals of providing generally high-interest nonfiction texts for all readers. We think upper elementary readers of all levels will find texts they'll feel excited about reading in these shelves. We especially wanted below-benchmark readers to be able to research extreme weather. Luckily, this topic is thrilling for children at all ages, so it was not hard to find books at a variety of levels on weather-related topics.

Then, too, there are books by Seymour Simon, beloved nonfiction author, as well as reliable favorites from the True Book Series, National Geographic Kids, DK Readers, Epic Disasters, and others. And students reliably gravitate toward *Weather Infographics; Boy, Were We Wrong About the Weather!*; and *Volcano! The Eruption and Healing of Mount St. Helens*—engaging and award-winning picture books that add nice variety to this shelf.

These shelves pair very well with the Grade 4 Reading Unit of Study, *Reading the Weather, Reading the World* (Heinemann 2015). During this unit, readers are asked to recognize text structures, synthesize content, and compare and contrast across texts, growing ideas as they read. To that end, the books on these shelves represent a variety of text structures and types. At each level, there is the possibility of creating mini-text sets so students can read up on one type of extreme weather or read across weather patterns, affording opportunities for readers to become more expert on various topics and more critical readers. We also included exciting topics not specifically highlighted in the unit, like volcanoes and forest fires.

Argument and Advocacy Shelf: Researching Debatable Issues (Grades 5 and 6)

Curated by Kelly Boland Hohne

The Argument and Advocacy Shelf consists of sets of books grouped around debatable issues. For each issue, the selection of books offers different perspectives and information on the topic.

There are a few ways in which this shelf's groupings tend to differ from those in the high-interest nonfiction books in the complete grade-level Classroom Libraries. There, books were chosen so if a child read a book on the undersea world, for example, he could also reach for a book on sharks and one on whales. Here, the child will have a chance to read different sides of the question: Should marine shows include killer whales? The books are grouped around a central debatable issue, rather than fitting under the umbrella of a bigger topic.

Within each set, or group, of books, some more explicitly address sides of the central debatable issue than others. That decision reflects the knowledge that kids, like adults, should always be willing to deepen their background knowledge about an issue as they research it. While one text might explicitly argue that killer whales kept in captivity do not live as long as whales in the wild, another text might give a lot of information about the hunting habits and distances that killer whales travel in the wild, and the reader needs to figure out what side of the debate this information supports.

One way that argument texts become harder is that the ideas the author promotes will be implicit. These texts set your readers up to not only read across an issue, but also to read up levels of complexity. You'll see that some of these texts are explicit and obviously on one side of an issue, some are more nuanced and introduce both sides of an issue, and some are more implicit, and the reader needs to analyze and infer to glean support for one side or the other. This is all fantastic reading work, and it's hard to do without text sets on hand.

It is important to note how this Argument and Advocacy Shelf differs from the kind of persuasive shelves we might have built five or ten years ago, before the influence of argumentation in the Common Core (whether we liked it or not!) pushed us to consider more deeply the difference between persuasion and argument. In persuasion, the researcher feels free to only research one side of an issue, and when writing and talking about that issue, to only include evidence to support that side. In argumentation, the researcher has to initially be willing to suspend judgment, read about the issue in general, and remain open to multiple perspectives and to complexity. These sets will help students practice the latter, which is a significant skill set to use in the world, as well as academically.

If you teach the *Argument and Advocacy* unit (Heinemann 2015) and/or the *Research-Based Argument Essays* unit (Heinemann 2013) from the fifth-grade reading or writing Units of Study, the sets in this shelf will help you organize students into research and debate clubs so they can pursue collaborative research. The shelf includes sets of books around these eight issues, which are framed here as debate questions:

- Extreme sports: worth the risks?

- Plastic bags: should they be banned?

- Killer whale shows: should they be banned?

- Mount Everest: should it be climbed?

- Sharks versus humans: who is in more danger from whom?

- Exploration: should it be underwater or outer space?

- Zoos: should we support them or ban them?

- Plastic water bottles: a force for good?

To be included, a book had to accomplish at least one of three things (often it did more than one): directly address the issue and explain the argument, offer background information that could help students to talk about an issue with more authority and understanding, and/or help raise new questions related to aspects of the larger issue. Some sets, such as extreme sports, include more texts at easier levels. As you browse these, think of your students' interests and their levels. There should be something for everyone.

Dive in. Expect to be interested, outraged, and stirred to action!

Book Club Shelves

After choosing 180 fiction books or one hundred fantasy books for fifth-graders for our classroom libraries, we thought it might be a breeze to home in on just twelve or so books for book clubs (offered in sets of four). We were surprised that most book club shelves required days of reading, talking, thinking before final decisions were made. These were some of our considerations:

- Books that are read by clubs need to be especially talk-worthy. We looked for books that invited close reading, conversation, rereading, and writing about reading.

- We anticipated that teachers would keep the sets of book club books out of regular circulation, which may be a problem for popular series. On the other hand, if the club is meeting early in the year, it could conceivably be a perfect way to launch a series, as long as that series is one not likely to be critical in the preceding year.

Books that are read by clubs need to be especially talk-worthy.

- Book club members will generally read a sequence of books, and will talk between those books. It is helpful, then, if this shelf of books contains several books at similar levels of text complexity that explore the same theme, setting, or plot outline in different ways and therefore invite comparison.

- We know that book clubs might be composed of boys, girls, or a mix, and therefore titles chosen for book clubs need to appeal to both genders.

- If a group of students reads a set of books across time, it is important that the set contains something for everyone. For instance, if one book is characterized by high adventure, another might be more of a relationship book. We worked for diversity across the books at each text level, and that includes racial diversity and a variety of settings.

- If there are four books in a club set that are written at similar levels of text complexity, we generally anticipate that more than one club will probably delve into those books, with different clubs progressing through those books in a different sequence. This, and the fact that we expect many teachers will already have sets of a few books, explains why we calculated that twelve titles (with a few exceptions) may be a sufficient number.

Character Book Club Shelves (Grade 3, Below-Benchmark and On-Benchmark)

Curated by Kristin Smith and TCRWP Classroom Library Project Leaders
When creating the Character Book Club Shelves, we searched for books in which the characters come alive and have unique, strong, noteworthy traits. We hoped to find characters who change through a story. In some ways, it was easy to find candidates for these shelves, and the challenge was limiting the list. (We ended

up including thirteen titles in the Below-Benchmark Shelf.) Beloved characters like Poppleton, Stink, Mallory, and Jamaica quickly came to mind. We knew children would love reading and thinking about their vibrant personalities. You'll notice the third-grade below-benchmark character book clubs introduce readers to some beloved early series book characters, such as Horrible Harry, Arthur, Iris and Walter, and Froggy. We intentionally included those books. We fear that often below-benchmark readers miss out on meeting the most cherished characters because their reading levels don't match with the grade level where these characters are featured.

However, in both these book club shelves, we also wanted to include characters who are new to us, and we think, to students and teachers, too. In the third-grade below-benchmark Character Book Club Shelf, we feature Benny and Penny from Toon Books, publisher of graphic novels illustrated by famous cartoonists like those featured in *The New Yorker* magazine. In the third-grade benchmark Character Book Club Shelf, we included a story from the Nikki and Deja series about two best friends whose dilemmas are relatable to third-grade students. We also included a Roscoe Riley story, a character from the great author, Katherine Applegate. Roscoe Riley is a character whose crazy schemes always seem to land him in trouble.

We hope that within these book club shelves, all readers will find characters that are as interesting as the people in their own lives.

Historical Fiction Book Club Shelves

Curated by Shana Frazin

Selecting the Historical Fiction Book Club books was much more complicated than choosing the single copies of this genre. Try to picture a group of readers, reading at roughly the same reading level. We needed to get several books at this level of text complexity for those readers, and also set in the same historical time period. When choosing several books about a shared time period, we also wanted to select novels that would be rich for club conversation, worth reading interpretively and discussing deeply.

If you are teaching *Historical Fiction Clubs* (Grade 4) from the Units of Study for Teaching Reading (Heinemann 2015), this unit of study channels readers to read between fiction and nonfiction. We aimed to do that here as well, making sure that each nonfiction text we included illuminates the time and place in which the historical fiction stories are set. For all these reasons, these shelves each contain fewer titles on specific topics.

As an example, here are the texts we selected for the Grades 4–5 Segregation and Civil Rights club of S/T readers:

In the Year of the Boar and Jackie Robinson by Bette Bao Lord

Glory Be by Augusta Scattergood

Shooting the Moon by Frances O'Roark Dowell

Jackie and Me by Dan Gutman

Freedom Summer by Deborah Wiles

Dad, Jackie, and Me by Myron Uhlberg

Protest! How Americans Changed History by Emily Rothschild (nonfiction)

We suggest you encourage readers to orient themselves to the text set they will be reading as a club. After studying the novels, picture books, and information books that comprise the set, club members will probably want to make a reading plan for what they will read first, next, and after that.

For example, for the texts listed above, you might suggest that the club begin with Dan Gutman's *Jackie and Me*. In this book, a part of the Baseball Card Adventure series, Joe Stoshack uses an old Jackie Robinson baseball card to travel through time to complete his school assignment to write about a famous African American. You might think, "Time-travel fiction is not historical fiction." However, we included time-travel fiction because it supports kids in bridging the gap between their own lives and the past.

After reading this text, the club could gather around the remaining titles, studying the covers, back blurbs, and the layout of the chapters, and they could discuss which text to read next. Perhaps one reader might argue that reading *The Year of the Boar and Jackie Robinson* next might make sense because readers could compare and contrast how each author told the story of Jackie Robinson and his journey to desegregate baseball. Another club member might notice that both the picture book, *Freedom Summer*, and the novel, *Glory Be*, address segregation in the 1960s. That member might suggest reading chronologically, following a timeline to compare and contrast events in the late 1940s and the early 1960s. Your readers will no doubt be full of ideas for when and how to read the informational text,

Protest! How Americans Changed History, to further develop their conversations and comprehension.

Fantasy Book Club Shelves (Grades 4–5, Below Benchmark and On-Benchmark)

Curated by Katie Clements, Eric Hand, and TCRWP Classroom Library Project Leaders

The Fantasy Book Club Shelves include many of our favorites, culled from classrooms we support around the world. We prioritized texts by prolific authors and by authors who write across a variety of levels. That way, a child who falls in love with *Moongobble and Me: The Weeping Werewolf* by Bruce Coville can later read his books written at higher levels of text complexity, such as books in A Magic Shop series. A child who falls in love with *Catwings* can use the club as a launch into reading other favorite titles by Ursula LeGuin. We also decided to prioritize series, in hopes of hooking your students on Rowan of Rin or How to Train Your Dragon.

We've prioritized titles that include typical fantasy tropes: battles of good versus evil, heroes, quests, magic, and more. You could use these books in a study of symbolism or of interpretation, or in social issues book clubs, but they are especially aligned to the Grade 5 unit, *Fantasy Book Clubs: The Magic of Themes and Symbols*, part of the Units of Study for Teaching Reading (Heinemann 2015).

Interpretation Book Club Shelf (Grades 4–6)

We tried to locate books that both teachers and kids will love, and themes that provide wonderful cross-text conversations.

Curated by Alexandra Marron

When curating books for the Interpretation Book Club Shelf, we aimed to include books that supported close, deep, thoughtful interpretation reading. There are lots of fifth-grade books that have been favorites for teaching about theme, symbolism, and the like, and we included a few. But we wanted to introduce teachers and kids to books other than *Bridge to Terabithia*, *Holes*, *Wringer*, and *Sarah, Plain and Tall*, as wonderful as they are. To do this, we chose books such as *Out of My Mind*, *Last Summer with Maizon*, and *Rascal*.

One of our goals has been to locate books that both teachers *and* kids will love, so we tried to avoid some teachers' favorites (and our favorites) that kids seemed to be less fond of. We avoided other books because they didn't seem equally engaging for both genders. We weren't confident that a club of boys could be lured to love Judy Blume's *Are You There God? It's Me, Margaret*. We also avoided a few books because their themes didn't fit easily alongside other books in the shelf. A notable example was *The Lion, the Witch and the Wardrobe*.

We thought about themes that linked books and tried to choose a small selection of books at particular levels of text complexity that would provoke wonderful cross-text conversations, but we were also careful to not choose texts that were similar in narrow and literal ways. That is, we avoided selecting three texts about losing someone, for fear that readers might be channeled into seeing that as a single unifying theme. Our intention was that each sequence of books offers multiple ways to be interpreted and compared. We also imagined multiple ways to group the texts on the shelf.

Far and away the biggest challenge, however, was that of locating books at the lower levels of text complexity. It was not easy to find level Q and even R books that merited close interpretive reading and that supported this work across texts. At those levels, the texts tend to be action packed and fast paced (for good reason), and many didn't offer the depth that we want to support interpretation work. We included a few strong choices and hope to continue to search for more great options.

Chapter 5

Leveling Books, Assessing Students, and Matching Readers to Books

The Debate about Leveling Books and Matching Readers to Books

Even the wisest, most informed educators disagree on whether teachers should assign levels to books, identifying those levels with stickers on the front covers and perhaps organizing the library into leveled baskets. Good teachers disagree on whether to channel youngsters to read books at particular levels.

Those who disagree with book-leveling practices argue that the challenges a book poses to its readers vary based on a reader's prior experiences. A reader with a pet hamster might well be able to read a book about hamsters—perhaps even one about rodents—that would otherwise be too hard for her. Then, too, these people argue that slotting books into A–Z categories turns reading into something reminiscent of the SRA kits of our childhood. Students end up defining themselves as a level, saying, "I'm a 'Q,'" rather than defining themselves by genre ("I'm a fantasy reader") or by author ("Kevin Henkes is my favorite author") or by passion ("I love books about deep sea creatures").

Those of us at the Teachers College Reading and Writing Project take those concerns seriously, agreeing that there are problems to any leveling system. We recognize that across the globe, there are respected educators who differ from us on the topic of leveling books. We welcome dissent on this issue, and believe that in the end, school communities need to make their own decisions. We are confident that in many schools that downplay book levels and track kids' progress along trajectories of text complexity, teachers and kids have internalized the most helpful parts of the knowledge base. Instruction is still deeply informed by a knowledge of text complexity levels and by a commitment to helping youngsters engage in high-success reading.

Nevertheless, you will see that we have leveled the vast majority of books in this library. We'd like to take the opportunity to explain why we did this and to discuss the implications for instruction and assessment.

First, a caveat. A gigantic proportion of the books that we reviewed had not been leveled by Fountas and Pinnell. To construct the libraries with a distribution of book complexity that would match the readers at specific grade levels, we needed at least a tentative level on the books.

To arrive at text levels, we agreed to not rely on Lexile, even though Lexile levels are very easy to determine. The reason that they are easy to determine is also the reason that they are not rich enough to be very helpful: because Lexile levels are based solely on word and syllable counts, they do not take into account any other kinds of complexity. This can lead to absurdity. For example, Judith Viorst's charming but simple picture book, *Alexander and the Terrible, No Good, Very Bad Day* has a Lexile level of 950, which puts it in the grades 6–8 band, according to the CCSS. Meanwhile, Ernest Hemingway's classic, complex love story, *The Sun Also Rises*, has a Lexile level of 610, squarely in the grades 2–3 band. Clearly, using Lexile alone to determine the appropriate challenge level of these works would be foolish.

We did research whether a book had been leveled by *any* locatable system, such as Book Wizard, Scholastic, or Booksource. We took those levels into account, but if we had the book in hand (as we almost always did), we did not trust levels assigned by systems other than Fountas and Pinnell over our own judgment.

We have leveled the grades 3–8 books "in pencil," so to speak. We are aware that we do not have PhDs in leveling. There are others who have spent more time leveling and are more knowledgeable about text levels. In fact, we spent time questioning whether it would be helpful or not to share our tentative levels at all, as we cannot stand by them as definitive. In the end, we decided that our knowledge of reading development and of the particular texts is apt to be far deeper than the knowledge a busy teacher can draw upon when she is left to her own leveling resources so we have included our tentative levels of texts in the online resources and lists of the books packaged with each shelf.

You may wonder if the fact that we have assigned levels to books and included little stickers that ascribe levels means that we stand firmly in the camp of believing that the books in a classroom library should all be leveled. The answer is that, no, we aren't firmly in one camp or another. Instead, we think that teachers within a school should make the decision together as to whether it is helpful and important to level many of the books within your classroom libraries or not. If the decision is made to level books, it helps if teachers across a school do so in a coordinated fashion, using a single universal leveling system, and we suggest that the Fountas and Pinnell leveling system is most helpful to kids.

Still, the question remains: "Why level?"

There is a compelling body of research that suggests students benefit from reading books they can read fluently, accurately, and with basic levels of comprehension. A staggering percentage of kids come into classrooms each year without a sense of what reading is supposed to feel like when it is working. Therefore, many youngsters may not be able to monitor if a book is making sense to them. And even those who can gauge whether a book is appropriate for them or too hard, end up spending too much time on the deflating experience of starting one book, then giving it up, starting another, another.

We've come to believe, therefore, that it is helpful to provide students with a system of supports that can help them to select books that are apt to be within reach for them. We find that levels of text complexity can function a bit like markers on a ski trail. Coming off the chairlift, the skier can decide whether to head to a green circle trail or to a double diamond, and adults can use those markers to guide choices: "You can ski a few last runs without me, but no double diamonds, please."

A skier's knowledge of the trail markers and what they signify can exert more or less control over what the skier does. Perhaps the skier's knowledge that a trail will be challenging doesn't prevent that person from taking that trail, but does suggest the person may need support: a buddy or a forewarned parent. The skier can say, "If I am not at the lodge by noon, come after me with a toboggan." In the same way, when books are coded with letters that signal their level of text complexity, readers can gauge the sorts of supports they need to tackle a particular text.

From A to Z: Assessing Readers Using Fountas and Pinnell's Leveling System

The reading levels we use come from Irene Fountas and Gay Su Pinnell's work. They span from level A to Z+ and represent a gradient of ways that books become more complex, from a very beginning level to adult texts. For more information on reading levels, you might read *Leveled Books, K–8: Matching Texts to Readers for Effective Teaching* by Irene Fountas and Gay Su Pinnell.

The leveling system will only be useful if you also use running records to determine the level of text complexity that your readers can just handle. There are a variety of materials available that support teachers in conducting running records. Fountas and Pinnell have produced a boxed set for this purpose. Alternatively, your school may have versions of the DRA or the QRI. The Teachers College Reading and Writing Project website offers running records as a free download, although for your level A through L readers, you'll need to purchase a set of books from the publisher, as you can't effectively assess those readers from a printed-out text. The tools on the TCRWP website aren't better; they're just shorter and free of charge. In the end, all of these systems essentially accomplish the same task.

When conducting running records, a teacher asks a child to read up a ladder of increasingly difficult texts. Within a few minutes, you get a snapshot of a child's fluency, accuracy, and literal inferential comprehension with texts on a particular level of text complexity. You can then track how these change as the youngster tackles progressively more challenging texts. For teachers who have learned to analyze running records, this assessment tool provides a window into what's happening in a child's mind—information that can guide teaching decisions. Even without that deeper knowledge, however, running records can help you and your children know how they are progressing as readers.

Some may critique these assessments as reductive—and of course, describing a reader by identifying the level of text difficulty that the child can independently handle is not a sufficiently rich description of that child's reading. But as one component of a system of reading assessment and instruction, it does provide schools, teachers, and caregivers a leg up as they work to identify needs and ensure success for each student. For more information about implementing running records in your classroom, if you are using the Units of Study for Teaching Reading (Heinemann 2015), you may with to consult *Reading Pathways: Performance Assessments and Learning Progressions, Grades 3–5*.

You will want to assess other ways in which youngsters grow as readers, as running records do not provide information about a child's fluency, ability to read critically, to interpret, to compare and contrast, or to do a lot of other important skill work. The Units of Study for Teaching Reading provide performance assessments that give a great deal more information and help you keep your eye on a child's higher-level comprehension.

> *Leveling can be a helpful part of a support system to help students select books they can read accurately, fluently, and with basic conprehension.*

To use running records effectively, we believe it is essential that you norm the way teachers across your school assess running records. A quick introductory course on giving running records is also helpful. Many small decisions are made when conducting a running record: What percentage of comprehension questions must be answered correctly to pass? Is a repeated miscue counted once or every time? Taken together, these judgments can have an enormous impact on the progress students make class-wide and can impact their trajectory as they move through grades. If you are using the Units of Study for Teaching Reading, please see *Reading Pathways: Performance Assessments and Learning Progressions, Grades 3–5* for more information on schoolwide running records implementation.

A Book's Level of Text Complexity Suggests the Work Its Readers Need to Do

Your knowledge of levels of text complexity and of a particular book's level will be very helpful as you work with students. Once you know, for example, that a book is a level R, that can signal that even if you do not know that particular book, chances are good that you'll know the specific kinds of work a level R text will ask a reader to do—just from your knowledge of the text level. So if you pull your chair alongside a child who is reading a level R book (or a book at any other level), you draw on your knowledge of text complexity to be able to say something like, "I know that in many books at this level, readers keep on getting to know more about the setting as they read on. Can you walk me through what you knew early on about the place where this book is set? And then tell me some newer things you've been learning about the book's setting as you read?"

At the Teachers College Reading and Writing Project, we have found that it is not especially helpful for a teacher to try to memorize fifteen descriptors of books at levels A–Z. The differences between one level and another, especially as one gets higher in the text levels, are not that clear-cut. But we do find that there are some very clear-cut, helpful distinctions between what we have come to call "bands of text complexity." We have found that you can cluster levels of text complexity as follows:

K/L/M

N/O/P/Q

R/S/T

U/V/W

We have worked hard to develop the shortest possible list of characteristics for any one band of text difficulty and to talk about the work readers are required to do in language that does not require a PhD in reading instruction to be understood.

What kind of work is called for in band K/L/M?

(*Nate the Great* to *Captain Awesome*)

STRUCTURE

Books in this band tend to have one clear central problem and solution. Or, they tend to have one clear central problem and a resolution.

CHARACTERS

The characters have a few dominant characteristics, and these are explicitly labeled, repeatedly. "Horrible Harry is horrible!" The characters tend to be relatively static. They change their feelings over the course of the story, but their traits remain fairly consistent throughout the book.

VOCABULARY AND SYNTAX

Readers of books in the K/L/M band of difficulty are required to tackle an increasing number of two- and three-syllable words. They will find more and more words that are not the words they use conversationally—and many of them will be subject-specific. A story about soccer will include *opponent*, *cleat*, *faceguard*, and *positions*, for example.

What kind of work is called for in band N/O/P/Q?

(*The Chocolate Touch* and A to Z Mysteries series to *Fudge-a-Mania*)

STRUCTURE

Texts in the N/O/P/Q band of text difficulty are more structurally complex. The narrative frame is still present, but the character encounters not just one concrete problem but a blend of pressures, or a multidimensional problem. This means that between a character's motivation and the story's resolution, there will be a few subplots.

CHARACTERS

In addition to the more complex story line, the main character, or protagonist, will also tend to be more complicated. The character is often conflicted. Feelings tend to be ambivalent, and at least some of the trouble in the story is internal, related to these ambivalent feelings. The characters are complex, but readers are told about this complexity. Usually, it will not be subtle. Someone—the character or the narrator—will come right out and tell the reader the traits of the main characters.

VOCABULARY AND SYNTAX

At this band of text difficulty, readers encounter not just tricky *words*, but tricky *phrases* and tricky *passages*. Usually these are tricky because they include a play on language, perhaps a pun or a metaphor or a figure of speech. So at these levels, students will start to encounter figurative language and especially, non-literal language.

What kind of work is called for in band R/S/T?

(*Because of Winn-Dixie* to *The Tiger Rising* and *Bridge to Terabithia*)

STRUCTURE

In this band, there is a trend toward stories becoming layered with meaning. The characters and the events, too, are kind of like icebergs—with the part that shows, which is labeled and discussed, being only part of what's really going on. The problem may seem to be the relationship between two characters, but deep down, the problem is a bigger sense of loneliness (or another big issue). The problems are big enough and layered enough that they are not all solved. In fact the storyline is less about a character who encounters a problem and rises to the challenge, solving the problem, and more about characters who encounter problems and work to respond to those problems, changing and learning in the process.

CHARACTERS

The trend toward complexity grows in this band, and increasingly, the characters have complex internal, emotional lives. This often means that the characters are gray—both good and bad, more than one way. Minor characters become more important. Readers have to pay attention to how the minor characters influence and teach the reader about the main character.

VOCABULARY AND SYNTAX

Books in this band of text difficulty often contain tricky chapters. A teacher might say to these readers, "Before, if you came to a tricky chapter and were totally confused, you might think the book was too hard for you. Now, at this level, you need to expect that sometimes books are hard on purpose, and you are not supposed to entirely get what is going on. You can say, 'Huh?' and read on, expecting things will become clearer as you go."

What kind of work is called for in band U/V/W?

(*Loser* to *A Wrinkle in Time*)

STRUCTURE

In this band, there are many more complex structures in the books. A story may start with a flashback or a prologue in italics and then back up to start the main story. Readers have to figure out why that beginning part was included and how it relates to the story and the themes. As mentioned, there usually tends to be something important that happened before the story started that influences the story as it unfolds. There can also be more jumps in time within the story. There may be more foreshadowing of events to come—a later action or a new character coming.

CHARACTERS

Not surprisingly, the characters continue to become more complex and nuanced—but something else begins to happen at this level. Increasingly, the characters are teenagers. If the reader herself is not yet a teen, she can sometimes have a hard time empathizing with the characters. Also in this band, the point of view starts to become even more multidimensional. It starts to be not just interesting but necessary to consider the perspectives of characters other than the protagonist.

Helping Students Choose Just-Right Texts

If your students are new to independent reading and choosing just-right books, you might teach a minilesson early in the year about how to select books that are just right. To do this, you could pull out a little stack of books and demonstrate how you choose a book that is just right. Perhaps the first book you pull out from the pile is too easy, the kind of book you would have read years before. "This book is probably too easy for me," you might say. "It's the kind of book I might read on vacation as a beach read, but I'm not sure it will help me get stronger as a reader."

Next, you might pull out a thick book and dramatize how you struggle through it, reading a bit aloud and miscuing on several words on the first page as you read. "Whew, this book is just *too hard*," you might say, "because I don't have *a clue* what's going on here. I'll have to save this one for later." Finally, you might pull out a within-reach book and show students how you determine that this book is just right: it's one you can read smoothly, without many miscues on the page; it's one you understand well; and it's one you are interested in reading. Then, you could rally students to try the same thing, reading a chunk of a text and working to determine whether it's too easy, too hard, or within reach.

Then, too, you might choose to use some of your one-on-one time with students to ensure they're matched well with books. You might ask a child to read aloud a little of his book to you, then pause him and say, "Can you tell me a bit about what's happening in your book so far?" If the child has more than three miscues on the page or has trouble retelling the book, you might look to match that child with a more accessible text. Or, if you notice a child seems disengaged with a text, you might bring him over to the library and share three or four books or series you think might interest him. Your crafty salesmanship can really help get kids excited about a book!

How Can I Streamline Assessment at the Beginning of the Year?

Many schools find it is enormously helpful if, at the end of a school year, every teacher creates a baggie of books that travels with a child to the child's next grade. The year-ending classroom teacher works with the child to fill the baggie with an old favorite or two and with a batch of new books that promise to be just-right or easy (remembering that for children who do not read during the summer, there is always a slide backward) and as enticing as possible. That teacher can even coach children to plan their progress through one or two selected books. The teacher might use Post-its to mark the volume of reading to aim for on Days One and Two, relying on page-number patterns from the year ending to project progress through books in the year approaching. This system allows a teacher in September, who is assessing her incoming class, to watch those kids working with books that her colleague believed would be just right.

Meanwhile, this process allows this teacher's running records to be informed by a colleague's informal observations. More importantly, it means that every child can get started from Day One, reading books that have been carefully selected.

If that can't be done, hopefully last year's teachers will send along the end-of-year levels of text difficulty. And if even *that* can't be done, teachers in classrooms whose kids take end-of-year, high-stakes assessments will be able to access those test scores, which can provide a general guess as to the levels of text difficulty for incoming students.

In any case, once you have your new class and the children are reading texts that are roughly right for them, you can eyeball to see if youngsters are actually able to read those levels. Did they slip over the summer? If so, it may take just a very short while to get summer rust worn off and to be back to the levels at which they left off.

Professionals other than the classroom teacher can participate in conducting running records and matching readers to books. Many schools hire a reading specialist or others with special training in reading assessment to work with children during summer school or during the final two weeks of summer, conducting assessments and matching books to children. Some schools ask that these professionals conduct all the assessments for those who are particularly at-risk, thereby making it likely that these youngsters' time will be maximized, with every moment spent doing work that has been tailored to the child, and that their assessments will be as informed as possible. Other times, schools ask that summer assessments be given to a random sampling of children from every classroom, because having a few already-assessed children dotting a teacher's roster provides another way for classroom teachers to align their assessments with a schoolwide standard. At the very start of the year, some of the school's specialist teachers may not yet have their "specials" in place, so they might also be asked to help assess readers.

I also recommend that you and all your colleagues become accustomed to assessing students in groups, instead of one-by-one. That is, bring a cluster of children to the area in which you do assessments. Then explain what you'll be doing just once to that whole cluster, asking the children to sit near you and start their independent reading while you assess one child after another. You'll find that this increases the efficiency of your running records.

In the first weeks of school, the priority during your reading assessments is to help each child get access to a book—a stack of books really—that she can read. This is not the time to dive into conducting any one assessment in depth, discovering every detail of that reader's strengths, preferences, and needs. For now, it is more critical that you buzz through the whole class, conducting quick assessments that allow you to launch all students into reading just-right books—and, better yet, reading with a partner at about the same text level. If you get every child roughly assessed within the first two weeks of the school year, there will be time later to conduct more detailed, rigorous assessments and to follow up on all the questions that your initial assessments provoke.

What Do Running Records Look Like across the Year?

Your school will probably also want to establish that teachers conduct more formal running records at regular intervals across the year. As mentioned earlier, most schools we work with give running records at predetermined times at least four times a year for all readers—RTI requires five—and much more often for lower-level readers and children who read below grade level. Formal windows for conducting running records are quite common and have their advantages, but they also are problematic because it is common for teachers to only assess during those windows, and children often need to progress to new levels far more often than those four windows allow. If your students are reading up a storm, they will be ready to progress to new levels far more often than any formal whole-school assessment windows allow. For example, assuming you assess at the start of the year, you'll find that within a month, the summer rust will have worn off for many readers, and they'll be able to progress to higher levels. It is imperative, then, that assessing readers becomes no big deal.

At the start of the year, invite students to teach you who they are and what they care about as people and as readers and writers.

Give Children Many Ways to Define Themselves as Readers

Your first job at the start of the year is to fall in love with each and every student—right away. That is not always easy when you are still mourning the loss of last year's kids—and when you have multiple sections of students to get to know.

At the start of the year, I recommend that you find ways—straight away—to invite students to teach you who they are and what they care about as people and as readers and writers. During those first days of the school year, when no one is yet accustomed to sitting at a desk all day anyhow, it is important to set children up to represent their strengths and interests and quirks and habits as readers and writers. Perhaps you'll ask children to draw pictures of one time in their lives when reading was the best it could ever be and one time when reading was the worst ever—or to create a timeline of their reading lives.

The important thing will be the stories that children swap about their reading histories as they share their pictures. Perhaps you'll give each child a square of the bulletin board, and ask each one to bring in stuff that shows their histories as readers. That's a more powerful idea than you might think: imagine if you were asked to fill a square of the bulletin board with things that show *you* as a reader.

Which books, of all that you have ever read in your whole life, would you choose to put into that square? What ways of responding to reading would go there? It's not lightweight work to take the time to construct images of who we are as readers and to put those out into the world.

All of this work will allow you to begin to develop some language about how each of your readers is different from other readers. To one child, you might say, "You've got this way of reading and asking questions that gets to the heart of everything. It's such a special thing because your questions take us into deep conversations. I hope over the year, you teach us how you do that." The important thing to realize is that that child might be reading books that are the least complex of any books being read in the class, and yet the child is not just a reader who is working with that level of text. She is also an inquirer and a teacher of inquiry to the class.

My point is that you can temper the emphasis on a ladder-like progression of reading development if you highlight the many ways your students have composed reading lives for themselves. Each student is a complex combination of habits, aspirations, talents, preferences, and worries—far more than just a text level. Once you match kids to books, chances are good there will be talk such as, "I'm an N reader." You'll want to have the goods to broaden and balance that. "You are also our class expert on the sports page, aren't you? I can't believe that you actually read it every single day—and do that before you even come to school! You are going to have to teach the rest of us how to read statistics, 'cause I think most of us just ignore them. But you don't, do you?"

You have extraordinary power to make each child feel seen and respected—or to feel just the opposite.

Chapter 6

Teaching Methods

 Reading Aloud

Introduction

To fall deeply in love with reading, children need to first see and hear the sights, sounds, and rhythms of a book well loved. The single most important thing you can do to turn your class into readers, then, is to read aloud to them. Read aloud several times a day: read to greet the day, to bring a social studies inquiry to life, to teach about molecules or gravity, and to fall through the rabbit hole of story.

Above all, read aloud to immerse children in the glories of reading. "Read to them," Cynthia Rylant says. "Take their breath away. Read with the same feeling in your throat as when you first see the ocean after driving hours and hours to get there. Close the final page of the book with the same reverence you feel when you kiss your sleeping child at night. Be quiet . . . . Teach your children to be moved."

You may want to take time at the start of the year to read aloud bits of different books on your classroom shelves to give children a feel for the variety of voices, styles, and kinds of books. Read the opening of *Because of Winn-Dixie* and assume the spunky voice of India Opal Buloni. Then quickly shift gears to read the lyrical opening to *Home of the Brave* in Kek's solemn, conflicted voice. Then read a bit of a narrative nonfiction text, such as *Mesmerized: How Ben Franklin Solved a Mystery that Baffled All of France*, a beautiful, engaging picture book that teaches children about a little-known story from history that supports an understanding of the scientific method. Or read a bit of a biography, or a mystery, or a historical fiction novel. With each new snippet you read, use your voice, facial expressions, and reactions both to spotlight what's special about that book and to model your love of reading.

When you're reading aloud, you have the text, and the students don't. Otherwise, some kids are reading ahead, some are trying to catch up, and some are struggling with print. The point of read-aloud is to introduce fabulous texts and higher-level thinking, without reserving that work only for higher-level readers. By reading aloud, you make sure that kids' interaction with this text isn't mediated by their reading level. Later, you may copy excerpts from the text, for shared reading, or for any kind of closer study.

In a few days, you'll want to settle into a longer read-aloud, introducing it to your students with some fanfare. Each day after that, you'll gather your children together and read aloud a portion of that book, doing so in ways that model and invite the kind of reading you hope children do on their own. Part of this will mean sharing your responses to the book. Say things like, "I'm so excited for this chapter. All last night, I was itching to peek into our read-aloud so I could find out what happens next. Pull in close so we can begin!" Or "It's a rainy day! Don't you love reading on a rainy day? Come quick!" Or "I wonder what he's hiding in his pocket? I'm so worried! Aren't you?"

Soon, you and your children will gulp down stories—ones that invite you to paint colorful pictures with a gorilla at a shopping mall, to saddle up with a wannabe cowboy, to ride a bus across town and discover a world of people. Together with your kids, you will construct knowledge about weather forecasting and assemble a mental model of a weather station. You'll experience what it means to lose—and to find—yourselves in history, in a story. Word by word, chapter by chapter, you will be led into another time and another place and another field of study. "Great literature, if we read it well," Donald Hall has said, "opens us to the world and makes us more sensitive to it, as if we acquired eyes that could see through things and ears that could hear smaller sounds."

It won't be long before you begin to see your kids gasping at parts that surprise or move them, pulling a friend in to share a passage they love or a section that's taught them something memorable, laughing out loud when the text is funny, and crying when it is sad. They will have discovered what it is to fall deeply in love with a book—and with reading.

Choosing Books to Read Aloud

So how does one choose the texts to read aloud? Our advice is this: choose carefully. Spend your summer reading lots of books and carefully weighing your decisions. Consider texts that will open up new topics for your class. Consider texts that will bring your class together. Consider books that are too complex for your students to read on their own, books that can take your children toward more complex understanding of characters or settings or issues.

Think, too, about books that your struggling readers are reading. When you read a book such as *George and Martha* aloud, you use reading aloud and grand conversations to elevate the books and authors that are fundamental in the reading lives of these students.

Consider the length of books, too. If reading aloud is a mainstay in your classroom, by all means turn to powerful, complicated books such as *Brown Girl Dreaming, The Mostly True Adventures of Homer P. Figg,* or *Out of My Mind.* But if you have trouble finding twenty to thirty minutes a day for reading aloud, you'll want to opt for shorter books such as *Bink and Gollie, Crenshaw,* or *Dory Fantasmagory* so that your read-aloud doesn't drag on over too many days.

Your read-aloud anchors your minilessons, generally. When you teach a reading strategy, you'll be able to demonstrate it in the read-aloud text, which is already a familiar text. You'll need, therefore, to think about the relationship between your read-aloud books and your curriculum. Think about the relationship between the read-aloud and the topics of your content. If you weave a chapter book and a shorter text or two into a reading unit, building much of your instruction around that text, as we tend to do, your read-aloud of that chapter book will probably be held in check by the fact that particular parts of the book will be aligned to lessons you want to teach—and those lessons sometimes require prior work. You may want to maintain a second read-aloud in case the start of your main read-aloud doesn't showcase the content of your lessons.

You'll want to choose books for nonfiction read-aloud with equal care. Often, it's helpful to assemble a text set so that your read-aloud work will lead and mirror the work that children will do in their own texts. You'll also want to choose texts that are well written as well as informative, both so kids will fall in love with nonfiction and so that if you decide to study perspective or craft or structure, the text is rich enough to reward these lenses. Think, too, about how you'll layer texts in your read-aloud to build toward complexity. Children sometimes read nonfiction a level below the level at which they read fiction, so consider beginning with accessible, fascinating texts and gradually leading into more challenging ones. Most importantly, compare your read-aloud text choices to the texts your children will be reading, double-checking that the texts pose similar challenges. This mirroring of text complexity accomplishes two things. First, your read-aloud text will allow you to teach into these challenges and you can return to these texts during your lessons. Second, the work you do during read-aloud will either foreshadow or give children extra practice with work they need to do in their own texts.

Plan Your Read-Aloud: Start by Spying on Yourself While Reading, Then Forward the Skill Work You Do

To plan a read-aloud, it will help to first read the book (or the portion of the book) that you will be reading aloud to your children, spying on the work that you do as you read. Ideally, you'll do this in the company of some colleagues, talking together about the predictable kind of work a particular text supports. Say, for example, you decided to plan a read-aloud involving Roald Dahl's *Charlie and the Chocolate Factory*. Even if you have read the book before, you'd want to reread it and think about what your mind does as you read the text. It starts like this:

> These two very old people are the father and mother of Mr. Bucket.
> Their names are Grandpa Joe and Grandma Josephine.
> And *these* two very old people are the father and mother of Mrs.

Bucket. Their names are Grandpa George and Grandma Georgina.

This is Mr. Bucket. This is Mrs. Bucket. Mr. and Mrs. Bucket have a small boy whose name is Charlie Bucket.

This is Charlie.

How d'you do? And how d'you do? And how d'you do again?

He is pleased to meet you.

The whole of this family—the six grownups (count them) and little Charlie Bucket—live together in a small wooden house on the edge of a great town.

Ask, "What is the intellectual work I am doing? Is this work that readers often do when reading—or at least when starting—stories? Might I want to bring out this work in the read-aloud?"

For example, as I began this book, I was envisioning and predicting—two skills that I see as flip sides of each other and that are commonly asked for at the start of a book. I do think it is important for readers to be ready to read, envisioning the characters and their world, and so yes, I could imagine deciding to bring that work forward in a read-aloud.

To do so, I'd want to set readers up to be ready to listen to the read-aloud, envisioning. I might invite them to do this, and point out, "The good news is that these seven people—the two sets of grandparents, one set of parents, and Charlie, the main character—are even featured in illustrations." I'd show children the illustrations and invite them to use those illustrations to form initial impressions of what these characters are like, reminding them that always, readers develop hunches and then read on, with those hunches in mind, planning to correct or confirm them.

As you read on, you can continue to channel children to envision by noticing the envisioning you do and inviting kids to join you in this work. You'll find that the text steers you to pay attention to details about the setting, and you may say to your children, "When you start reading a book, the text will often give you details about the setting. It is helpful to know that the details about setting matter because they will give you insights into what the characters are experiencing."

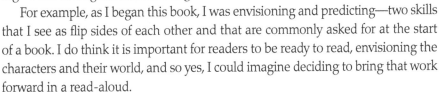

The house wasn't nearly large enough for so many people, and life was extremely uncomfortable for them all. There were only two rooms in the place altogether, and there was only one bed. The bed was given to the four grandparents because they were so old and tired. They were so tired, they never got out of it. Grandpa Joe and Grandma Josephine on this side, Grandpa George and Grandpa Georgina on this side. Mr. and Mrs. Bucket and little Charlie slept in the other room, upon mattresses on the floor.

After you read this passage, you might pause to think aloud, saying to kids, "Earlier, we learned that this family lives in 'a small house on the edge of a great town,' and now we are learning that the house isn't big enough for them all—in fact there's just one bed, which four people share! Although the text hasn't yet said as much, it is clear that this family is poor."

Soon your children will discover that for this family, there is never enough to eat; they are always hungry. The main character, Charlie, desperately wants "something more filling and satisfying than cabbage and cabbage soup." What he longs for above all is chocolate. And, more than that—what he's "tortured" by is the sight of Willie Wonka's chocolate factory, which he wishes with all his might to enter and see. That is, in the next few pages of the first chapter, the text will channel you and your students to begin to form an understanding of the main character's struggles and longings.

Making the Decision to Highlight Only Some Skills in Your Read-Aloud

Of course, while you spy on yourself reading even just a few pages, you will perhaps envision, predict, monitor for sense, make personal responses, ask questions, infer, develop theories about the characters, interpret, and so on. Although seasoned readers use a variety of skills simultaneously, for novice readers, it is easier to focus on a small cluster of related skills. So you'll need to decide which sequence of skills to highlight during the read-aloud.

> *Seasoned readers use a variety of skills simultaneously, for novice readers, it is easier to focus on a small cluster of related skills.*

After you decide to teach a cluster of three or four related reading skills, you will want to pass the read-aloud text through the sieve of just these skills. So say you decide to angle the read-aloud in ways that support envisioning and growing theories about characters. You'd then continue to spy on yourself as you read the text, but this time, you'd angle your reading work so that you especially did those things.

Let's revisit *Charlie and the Chocolate Factory*. Grandpa Joe, who eventually accompanies Charlie on his visit to Willie Wonka's chocolate factory, is a key character and an important person to Charlie. In Chapter 2, he makes his first big appearance. You might plan to angle your read-aloud of this scene to point out to your students that it helps to notice the entrance of a new character, and to use that entrance to recall if you already know a few things about that character.

Try this now, yourself. Imagine reading aloud Grandpa Joe's first line:

> "My *dear* boy," said Grandpa Joe, raising himself up a little higher on his pillow, "Mr. Willy Wonka is the most *amazing*, the most *fantastic*, the most *extraordinary* chocolate maker the world has ever seen! I thought *everybody* knew that!"

Pause for a moment and notice your reaction. You already know that Grandpa Joe is very old—soon you'll learn that he is "ninety-six and a half." Yet in this moment, he has the energy and enthusiasm of someone far younger. He describes Willy Wonka with such reverence and passion that it's impossible not to be caught up in this excitement yourself. Perhaps you're thinking that this Grandpa Joe is an unusual man.

Read on and you'll see that he continues to speak with animation and ardor. You might notice his tendency to emphasize words of praise like *magician*. By now you are forming an image of a man that doesn't match your image of most ninety-six-year-olds. You might wonder if Grandpa Joe is this lively all the time. Read on and you discover that it's *Charlie* who has this effect on him:

> But in the evenings, when Charlie, his beloved grandson, was in the room, he seemed in some marvelous way to grow quite young again. All his tiredness fell away from him, and he became as eager and excited as a young boy.

Now, perhaps, you think about the enormous love Grandpa Joe must feel for Charlie, to bring out this response in him—and you realize that in addition to passionate, this character is *compassionate*. He has a big capacity to love and to be invigorated by that feeling. Notice how your theory about Grandpa Joe, about a character, is growing. You are putting together—or synthesizing—information across pages to theorize about who he is.

Of course, as an experienced reader, you may also be thinking about how special a boy Charlie is; you may be envisioning and making predictions about this wondrous Willy Wonka and his factory, but shelve those thoughts for now. For the moment, stick solely to highlighting the specific skills you want to teach—developing theories about a character and synthesis.

As you read on, you'll find that not only is Grandpa Joe animated and passionate, he's also a storyteller. This is a man who weaves together tales with such elaborate detail and animation that everyone—the other characters and you, the reader—gets lost in his descriptions, in images of "little feathery sweets that melt away deliciously the moment you put them between your lips" and "lovely blue birds' eggs with black spots on them" that grow smaller and smaller in your mouth until all that's left is "a tiny little pink sugary baby bird sitting on the tip of your tongue."

Though first impressions often endure, developing a theory about a character across the story arc usually requires readers to *revise* their first impressions about the character. You'll point out to readers that it is helpful to read on, armed with Post-its or flags, ready to sift through the upcoming text, this time picking up and marking off the parts that add to a theory of who Grandpa Joe is. Along the way, you might plan to tell kids, "Even though he's very old—bedridden, even—he's got a sharp mind and a lively imagination. Characters are complicated. They aren't just one way."

Read-alouds are an enormously powerful tool in teaching reading because they dramatize—and make visible—the internal work of proficient reading. Teachers who read aloud most effectively *become* their character and enter the story. Practice being Grandpa Joe. Take on the voice of this man who loves words and stories and Mr. Wonka and above all, his grandson, Charlie.

Reading Aloud across the Curriculum

What a powerful tool this is to bring to science and social studies! Narrative reading can be exhilaratingly close to actually experiencing. Children learn that they can climb into the character or subject, whether that is a caterpillar as it eats its way out of its cocoon to become a butterfly, experiencing the thrill of metamorphosis, or George Washington, gathering his weary troops on a wintry Christmas morning, trying to inspire the men to stay with him.

You'll certainly want to bring this magic to expository nonfiction as well as to narrative nonfiction. You can read expository texts aloud in ways that highlight specific text structures—state the boxes in a stronger tone and then count out bullets on your fingers. Or, motion one way and another with your hand, wherever similarities and differences in a text are enumerated. You might read aloud a part and then stop to restate its main idea to the side. If your instructional focus is on synthesis and retelling, you might say, "Let's listen to this next part and see if it adds onto what we just learned or if it is a whole new thing." After reading a bit, you could say, "Let's pause. I do that when I'm reading expository nonfiction and my mind is full, don't you? Let's see if we can collect what we have learned so far."

Making Read-Aloud More Interactive

Reading aloud in a way that is spellbinding is an acquired talent, one that requires practice and planning. The teachers who are best at the art don't need to rehearse the thump-bump scary parts, the balloon-floating happy parts, and the slow, sad, knot-in-the-throat parts, as their reading aloud is an extension of their reading itself. These teachers use their hands, their eyes, their posture, their voices, and their hearts to bring life to their reading aloud.

> *To optimize instructional potential, children need the chance to respond to the texts you read aloud.*

But no matter how thrilling your dramatic impersonation is, to optimize instructional potential, children need the chance to respond to the texts you read aloud. Imagine for a minute that someone were teaching you to drive. Think about what you can learn from riding with a proficient driver, hearing him explain why he's choosing to brake or accelerate, and what he plans to do at the upcoming intersection. But you also need to take your *own* spot behind that wheel, with that proficient driver beside you, advising and encouraging you when you enter the traffic flow.

To pass the baton to children, instead of pausing to think aloud as you read, you'll become adept at saying to your students, "Stop and think," and then leaving a pool of silence, or saying "What are you thinking? Turn and talk," sending children into partnership conversations. Sometimes, instead of saying "Turn and talk," you'll say, "Stop and jot," and duck your head to do this while kids do as well. Of course, there are many variations on these prompts. Instead of saying "Stop and think," you can say, for example, "Oh my gosh, what's going to happen next? Predict, will you? Make a movie in your mind of what will happen next." Then, after the pool of silence, "Let's read and find out." That is, any of these prompts can be made more specific. "Stop and jot" could be "Stop and jot. What's this *really* about?" or "Stop and summarize. What's happened so far?" Still, the three main invitations you'll give will be to think, to talk, and to write.

Each of these three prompts invites children to develop and articulate their own independent responses to the text, and each prompt does this in a different way. Silent thinking is the most introspective of the three methods and is perfectly suited for especially moving or poignant parts. The turn-and-talk incorporates a social element, allowing peers to model, imitate, or reinforce each other's ways of responding to text. The stop-and-jot differs from a written response by allowing children just a moment in which to scribble a few words, quickly catching the images or thoughts that bubble to the surface before they're dragged back into the flow of the continuing read-aloud.

When you plan, then, you'll think about not just the specific skills that you'll teach during a read-aloud and not just the *points* at which you'll nudge children into responding, but also about the various ways to scaffold their response—through silence, through talk, or through pencil and paper.

Of course, there will be days when you pause more or less or not at all. There will be other days and books that will invite—almost beg—questions, discussions, and hot debate. You and your children will decide which of those days and books are for your community. The best thing about a read-aloud is that it can be tailored to fit your time, needs, and instructional agenda. When done often and done well, it can be the binding cement that holds your community of readers together.

Supporting a Whole-Class Grand Conversation

When you finish reading for the day, you'll want to support your children in talking together as a class about the text. Whole-class conversations offer important opportunities to teach children to grow ideas about texts, to hold themselves accountable to what the text says, to mine passages for meanings that may not at first be apparent, to think across texts, and to use their higher-level comprehension skills.

You need to decide whether to channel the conversation in a particular direction or to let children develop an idea. Imagine you choose the latter. You'll close the final page of the chapter and say, "My mind is on fire. Isn't yours? Turn and tell your partner what you're thinking!"

As the children talk, you might crouch among them, listening in. After a few minutes, you convene their attention and start the whole-class conversation with an invitation. "Who can get us started in a conversation? Who's got an idea to put on the table?"

Later, you might take time to show children how to sift through their thoughts to find a thought that is provocative, compelling, and central to the text, and to think, "Will this thought that I have pay off? Will it be an important one to develop?" When readers become skilled at this, their conversations—and writing and thinking—about books will head toward interesting terrain.

In any case, once I have nodded to a child who signaled with a thumbs up that he could get a conversation started, I'll probably make sure that class members look at that child, giving him their attention. "All eyes on Tyrell," I might say, and signal for Tyrell to wait until he has his classmates' attention. I might also coach Tyrell to say his idea to them—not to me, not to his collar, and not to his hand held over his mouth.

He puts his idea out there. Now I want the others to ponder it, and I want the idea to spark thoughts. I'm apt to model the way I listen deeply, taking in the idea that someone else has put onto the table. "Hmm," I say, as if the idea is a new one, dawning on me as I reflect on it. I repeat it to myself aloud, making sure that my mind is going ninety miles an hour as I think about my response to that idea. I know that children can see and feel the wheels of my brain spinning, and I know that I'll help them think in response to this idea if I actually do so as well.

If I think the children don't have much to say in response to this idea yet, I'll give them a few minutes to develop some thinking. I might say, "Let's take a second and jot our thoughts about this, okay?" Then again, if I want to support children's thinking, I could suggest that instead of writing, they talk with each other. That means that in the end, if one of the two partners has a thought, that person can carry the other partner. If I want to be sure their ideas are text based, I might distribute copies of a relevant passage and channel students to annotate, then to talk in pairs, linking that passage to the ongoing conversation.

In any case, the whole-class conversation will soon resume, and I may need to pause to allow a student to add a new idea to the conversation: "All eyes on Joan." After Joan comments, if it looks like others plan to report back on their prior thinking rather than build a new line of thinking, I'll need to channel their thoughts. I'll then say, "Who can talk back to Joan's idea?" and I may reiterate that idea. If the next speaker addresses her comments to me, I'll signal that she needs to speak to the group and to the original speaker. Now a second related idea will be on the floor. I'll probably raise my eyebrows and scan the group, asking without words for someone to add on, and when one child catches her breath like she can hardly contain the idea that has come to her, I'll try to refrain from calling on her with words, using a gesture instead. I'm hoping that before long one child will speak and another and another, without me needing to emcee the entire conversation.

The Teachers College Reading and Writing Project website features a number of videos showing classroom conversations that result from this sort of instruction. With libraries as rich and as carefully selected as yours, you are positioned to have conversations that truly live up to the term, "grand conversations." Watch those videos, invite your kids to watch them as well, and then—go for it!

Independent Reading, Conferring, Small-Group Work, and Partnerships

Independent Reading

Our hunch is if we asked each of you, "What are you really after in the teaching of reading?" you'd answer, "I want my students to become lifelong readers."

Sometimes we say these words, not realizing that what we actually mean is, "You can judge my teaching by whether my students initiate reading in their own lives, whether they weave books into their lives with the people they know and the passions they feel." These are not small goals.

One of the oldest, simplest ways to do this is to embrace this belief: to support kids to become lifelong readers, give them access to high-interest books, time to read those books, a rich social life around the books, and explicit instruction in the habits, skills, and strategies of proficient readers.

PROVIDE STUDENTS WITH TIME FOR READING AND ACCESS TO HIGH-INTEREST BOOKS OF THEIR CHOICE

To make schools into places where youngsters thrive as readers, we need to clear out time and space so children can learn to read by *reading*. This means shoveling out the busy work. Speaking at Teachers College, Richard Allington said, with a twinkle in his eye, "*Crap* is the technical term reserved for all the non-reading and non-writing activities that fill kids' days—the dittos, dioramas, papier-mâché maps . . . all that chases real reading and real writing out of the school day" (2008). In the classrooms of exemplary teachers, students read and write ten times as much as kids in other classes.

Think of it this way. When you teach reading, you are teaching a skill, like playing the oboe or swimming. The learner learns by practicing that skill, not by listening to someone talk about playing the oboe or swimming. As Grant Wiggins said when he spoke at Teachers College, you don't learn to drive by taking a car apart and studying every tiny screw and cog that goes into the car. You need to practice driving. In the same way, your students need to practice the skill of reading.

A mountain of research supports the notion that teachers who teach reading and writing most successfully are those who provide their students with substantial time for actual reading and writing. Allington reports that exemplary reading teachers have their students reading and writing for as much as half the school day. In typical classrooms, it is not unusual to find kids reading and writing for as little as 10% of the day.

> *Teachers who teach reading and writing most successfully provide their students with substantial time for actual reading and writing.*

It is no small goal, then, to give students long stretches of time to read books they are able to read. In too many schools, a ninety-minute "reading block" includes no more than ten or fifteen minutes of actual reading (Allington 2002). Students in the classrooms of more effective teachers read ten times as much as students in classrooms of less effective teachers (Allington and Johnston 2002).

Research also suggests that both quantity and quality of reading material are important. In a study called "Does practice make perfect? Independent reading quantity, quality, and student achievement" (Topping, Samuels, and Paul 2007), data were collected on 45,670 students in grades 1–12. The results indicated that reading high-quality books in high quantity led to high academic achievement gains. The books you give to your students matter tremendously; they are among your most powerful tools.

SETTING UP INDEPENDENT READING: SCHEDULING, MATCHING READERS TO BOOKS, AND MANAGING

If your goal is to help children compose richly literate lives, then you need to give them time each day to do that. A reading workshop provides an opportunity for mentoring children in composing a literate life, for teaching children to choose just-right books and to monitor for sense, to carry books between home and school, to not have a lonely reading life, to read a second book by an author differently because they've read the first, to get and develop ideas from books. The reading workshop is the closest you come to seeing how your kids author their own reading lives. If you're not teaching into your children's independent reading lives—if you're not drawing from and giving to those lives—how can you be certain our teaching is affecting them at all?

In reading workshop, children watch each other swapping books, gossiping about characters, reading favorite passages aloud to friends, or searching for information on a hobby, and they say "I want that for myself." You'll see them reading quietly, jotting notes, underlining, and getting ready to defend their thinking. Others may be working on reading slightly more difficult texts, and you'll see them previewing the texts, using what they've learned about getting ready to read to orient themselves to the topic and the text structures. Still others may be working on teaching about what they've learned, and you'll see them giving each other mini-lectures about the topic, referring to what they've read, and using the charts and illustrations to highlight their teaching. Learners are willing and able to work on the particular parts of becoming stronger readers. Because they see literate life in action, they value it, and they consider this life as doable and worth doing.

Teachers who are beginning the reading workshop model, or who are even just providing students with time for independent reading, sometimes worry about management. Management matters, because in a well-managed classroom, youngsters are able to read with more stamina. One way to support classroom management is to channel some readers to find private reading nooks. Usually, at the start of the year, children read at their desks. Those who do not have difficulty staying engaged with a book are then encouraged to find a place in the classroom

where they can do their best work as a reader. Eventually, half the class may be reading at their desks (with empty seats beside them, which allows teachers to pull in easily to confer), while others each have a long-term "reading nook." With students spread across the classroom, it is easy for you to move from student to student or group to group for instruction.

Many teachers find it helpful to provide each student with a "book baggie" or "book bin." When children go to the classroom or school library and choose books, they put those books in their personal baggie or bin. This way, readers have a bunch of books "on deck," so when they finish one book, they immediately begin the next, without roaming around the classroom. This process of planned book selection supports engagement in sustained reading.

If your reading time begins with a minilesson or a read-aloud, afterward children can head off to read, carrying their books and their reading tools, such as bookmarks, Post-its, a reading conference record sheet, and a log of books they read. The log should reflect the progress that a child makes in a book when reading that book at school and also when reading that book at home. We recommend (or experts recommend) that children read for half an hour in school and an equal length of time at home. At reading level J, children should be able to read about three quarters of a page a minute, so on average children should read something like twenty pages in school each day and an equal amount at home.

Many teachers ask students to keep logs of their reading time and the number of pages read so that students can be held accountable for their reading volume. Teachers can hold themselves accountable, too, for providing kids with the opportunities and the expectations that make it likely they read a lot.

If a child is struggling to stay engaged in her books, chances are good that she is holding books that she can't actually read. Sit alongside that child and ask, "Where are you in the book?" and once the child has told you where he or she is, ask for a summary. "I haven't read that book. Can you tell me what's happening?" Listen with rapt attention and try hard to grasp the story from what the child says, asking a few questions so that you can follow her rendition. If you can't piece together the story's logic, say something like, "It seems a little confusing. Is this book a confusing one?" You really mean, "Is this book too hard for you?" but the child generally will find it is easier to disparage the book. "Yeah," she'll say. "It is a *really* confusing book." Then you have a pretty good indication that the book is too hard.

You will also want the child to read aloud to you. Just listen for intonation that shows the child gets what he or she is reading. It will be totally clear from the intonation alone. Does the child's reading sound like talk? Do the sentences sound sensible? Meanwhile, quickly count miscues. Is the child reading with 96% accuracy, at least? If not, the book is probably too hard, and you will want to match that child to a book that is within reach. The assessment chapter in this *Guide* will help with that.

The other challenge will be to help the child become engaged with a book. One of the easiest ways is to read the first chapter aloud to the child. Work together to discuss and put together what you are learning about the story and to generate some big questions that the text will answer soon. Better yet, perhaps you can pull in another child to read a second copy of the same book, and plans can be made for the readers to pause and talk about what they've read.

INSTRUCTION IN HIGH-LEVERAGE SKILLS AND STRATEGIES

There was a time when people championed DEAR time—drop everything and read. The idea was that teachers as well as kids would spend half an hour a day reading. Now more and more educators know that although time to read high-interest books is necessary, it is not sufficient. Students also need instruction.

We would never think of distributing math books to kids, turning down the lights, turning on the music, and saying, "Do math! Multiply!" In the same way, it is not enough to turn on the music, to bring out the pillows, and to invite kids to "Reeeeaaaad."

Other books, such as those that comprise the Units of Study for Teaching Reading, describe ways to teach the skills and strategies of proficient reading. At its core, what matters is that you read as well as you can, and you think about the mind work you are doing as you read, then you make a point to let kids in on that mind work. So you read a short story and the character fingers the rock in his pocket, and for you, it is as if the ominous background music has just begun. Tension builds, and you think, "Who is he going to hurt?"

It is important for you to realize that some kids read right past the rock in the pocket without any of that thinking. Your job is to let them in on the thinking that skilled readers do by deconstructing that thinking. The first step: you are reading merrily along, yes, but are you expecting something to go wrong? Probably. After all, this is a story. You know there will be a problem that happens—so tell your students. Let them know that at the start of a story, you aren't just gliding over the words. You know you need to do some work here, and you are reading with alertness, aiming to do that work.

To teach the skills and strategies of proficient reading, it is helpful to engage in your own reading and to notice how the mental work you do as a reader is different from what some kids are doing. To note the differences, you will want to understand kids' thinking. You might interview a reader, "Tell me, what are you thinking now?" You might develop performance assessments in which you embed questions into a text and ask the reader to jot his or her thoughts when those questions occur in the text.

You also will want to realize that the skills of proficient reading are not just book skills, they are life skills. Someone paddling a canoe across a lake as a storm rolls in will do work similar to skilled readers. She will search for clues and put things together, asking, "What might this mean?" She will forecast and carry on with the prediction in mind, looking for evidence that confirms or changes the theory. She will compare this day with other days. Knowing that reading skills are life skills gives you more ways to teach kids the skills and strategies of proficient reading. You can watch a film together, pause it and talk about interpretation. You can replay it and this time look for the ways the weather creates tone. You can slam the door of the classroom and pound into the room and ask kids to "read" our actions, and then engage them in a conversation about how they read the people in their lives and in their books.

Whatever skill or strategy you highlight with your kids, they can practice using what you have taught them with any book that they are reading. One child can be reading a Magic Treehouse book and another a Gary Paulsen book, both aware of craft moves that the author makes repeatedly, and both knowing it helps to pause and ask, "Why might the author be doing that?"

This means that when teaching the skills and strategies of proficient reading, what you need most is an awareness of your own reading—and lots of highly engaging rich books for your kids to read, read, read.

> *The teacher's job is to let students in on the thinking that skilled readers do by deconstructing that thinking.*

HELPING TO LIFT THE LEVEL OF YOUR STUDENTS' READING THROUGH CONFERRING

Teachers who have taught literature-based reading workshops find that holding one-to-one conferences with individual readers is almost as important as having one-to-one conferences with individual writers. If you are uncertain how to conduct such a conference, it may help to realize that you know a lot about conferring already—from other parts of your life, where you may have played the part of the student instead of the part of the teacher. For example, think of a time you have gone to an expert for guidance, for coaching. Perhaps you have gone to your minister, your rabbi, your doctor, your fitness coach, your principal, or your staff developer. When you went to that expert, how did you want the interaction to begin? My hunch is that you expect a question such as, "What have you been working on lately?" or "What sort of help could I give you?"

Your conferring will be much more powerful if you draw on memories of those interactions to guide you as you frame your interactions with your kids. The truth is that kids are not all that different from you and me. If a child has been reading and working on becoming a better reader, then it makes sense that you do some research before you can teach in a way that will make a difference. Chances are good that you'll begin your reading conference by asking something basic, such as, "How's it going?" or "What have you been working on as a reader?" or "What new work have you been doing as you read this?" Asking these questions is part of your research.

If you have had the good fortune of being asked that sort of question, you found what I have found. The question alone will have led you to reflect, to dig deep, and even sometimes to create dawning insights about yourself.

There are also times when someone asks, "What new things have you been working on?" and you respond in a perfunctory way. Maybe you sensed the person wasn't really interested. We all know there are ways in which a person can listen, leaning in to hear more, in ways that convey, "Say more," signaling for us to amplify what we've said, responding with gasps or little interjections that make us feel heard and understood. Those signals make us want to talk. A good reading conference begins with deep listening.

Your conference will benefit from prior information about that reader. For example, if you know a reader has been abandoning books shortly after starting them, you would not begin the conference by asking, "How's reading been going for you lately?" Instead, you might say, "I've noticed you started and stopped three books in the last few days. That's unusual for you. You aren't usually a picky reader. What's been going on for you?" Then, too, if you began a line of work during a

previous conference, you're apt to bring readers to that vicinity and to say, "Last time we met we talked about . . . How's that going for you?"

Channel the child to shift from telling to showing. So if the child says that she is collecting evidence to back a theory she has about a character, you could say, "Could you walk me through that work?" Alternatively, if the child doesn't have evidence of the work or is just about to embark on it, you could say, "So, will you get started doing that right now while I watch?" As the child sets to work, you can inquire, "I see you are skimming this page. What are you thinking?"

Remember that after following a line of questioning, you need to go back and start a second line of questioning. This will give you information for options on where to go next. Starting a second line of questioning can be as simple as asking, "One thing you have been working on is increasing your stamina. What else are you trying to do as a reader?" Then again, you can launch your second line of questioning differently. "Will you think about yourself as a reader? Have the last few days been a good streak for you as a reader, or so-so, or not too good?" Or you can say, "There are some things that we've been studying as a class. Can you talk to me about the work you have been doing around . . . ?"

Not only do you need to launch a second line of inquiry, but you also need to gather information from many sources. So as that child explains that he is reading *Poppleton* and working on his stamina, you will glance at his log. You'll note if he's been reading within this series for a while, and what he read before. You'll check on how many books he is reading in a day, and if he is reading at home. If you have taken running records recently, you glance at them and recall his sources of difficulty. You notice the writing about reading he has or has not been doing. All that information comes into your brain at the same time you pursue your second line of questioning. Often, what you see sparks that second line of questioning.

Inviting children to reflect on and articulate what they have been doing as readers allows them to verbalize their strategies, which is helpful for a number of reasons. This puts them in a position to teach you those strategies. Still, there will be times when a child can't name what he's doing as a reader, so you'll say, "Will you do that work right now, as I watch?" Then after the child does whatever it is—say, orienting himself to get ready to read an expository article—you can name what you have seen the child doing. "So to me it looks like you are the kind of reader who doesn't just pick up an article and sort of drift into reading it," I say, feigning a sleepy, passive approach to the text. "No way! You turn your mind on to high even as you just get the article into your hands. And it looks to me like when you look over the article, you are already thinking about what the big ideas might be that it will teach readers. Am I right?"

Abundant research shows that just *doing* a thing—just reading—is not the best way to accelerate one's development. Instead, it is through deliberate, goal-driven work that people improve at almost anything. Your questions can promote that conscious, deliberate, goal-driven approach toward reading.

It is important that a conference gives you the sense that you have the capacity to do the work, to rise to the occasion. If someone watches you teach or reads your rough-draft writing or studies the records of your reading or hears about your marriage or looks over your hair and then says, "Geez. This is a bigger problem than I realized. I don't know . . . ," then this one interaction can totally convince you that you are not cut out to be a teacher, a writer, a reader, a spouse, or a beautiful person. Marie Clay has written extensively about the fact that sometimes, without meaning to do so, we can actually teach children that they *can't* solve problems, *can't* help themselves, *can't* get better. Clay's classic paper, "Learning to Be Learning Disabled," shows that just as a teacher can help a child learn to be an active agent of his or her own learning, a teacher can also teach children to be passive victims, filled with self-doubts (Clay 1987).

After researching what a child has already done and has been trying to do, I try to do two interrelated, intertwined things. I decide what to teach the reader, and I compliment. Sometimes I compliment first, then decide, and sometimes the sequence is the reverse. But either way, I take a few moments to name what the child has already done that I hope he or she continues forever more, work that I hope becomes part of the child's identity. I think, "Out of all that I could possibly say and teach, what will help the most?"

Guard against the tendency to slip between a conference and the teaching part of the conference because I find that often, the reader doesn't even grasp that the conference has taken a turn. For example, if I complimented Kobe on his envisionments becoming more detailed and on working with resolve to accomplish that goal, and now I wanted to teach him to be more attentive to tone and mood in those envisionments, the best way to make my point wouldn't be to go from the compliments to ask, "Do you know what mood means? When you envision what's going on, do you think about the mood?" Instead, I'd ask

permission to teach him a tip. "Do you mind if I give you one small but important tip?"

When our teaching is especially subtle, kids often miss it. If we are not explicit, the chances that they learn something they can use again another day is unlikely. Once you tell a child your teaching point, your tip, you probably will want to show the child what you mean. You will probably carry with you the class read-aloud and a short stack of other books that your children are familiar with so that you're able to quickly say, "For example, let's read this page of this book that we were reading last week. This is the part where . . . I'm thinking . . . now let's read on together and see if we can . . ." Then you demonstrate and name what you have done in the demonstration that you hope is transferable to the kids.

The conference may turn as you say, "So try it," or it might end with you suggesting the reader try this not only today with this text, but often. You might give the reader some sort of a cue card or reminder—a bookmark, perhaps, containing a summary of what you've just gone over together, or a special color of Post-its to mark times when the reader does this over the next few days, making it easy for you to see the traces of that work. By then, it is time to record what you've taught and learned and to scurry on to another reader, another lesson—for the child, and for you.

HELPING TO LIFT THE LEVEL OF YOUR STUDENTS' READING THROUGH SMALL-GROUP WORK

The first and most important thing to say about small-group work is this: Do it! The good news is that while your kids are reading up a storm, reaping the bounties of your Classroom Library, you can easily pull together several small groups each day. You need to make leading a small group into no big deal.

Guidelines to Inform Your Small-Group Work
Here are a few tips that can generally help all of your small-group work:

- Choose what and how to teach. Don't try to teach the text, but instead, teach the reader something he or she could use another day, with another text. That is, teach a transferable skill or strategy.

- Keep your teaching short. Imagine that in a ten-minute small group, you are talking and demonstrating no more than two minutes.

- To effectively demonstrate, name the teaching point ("One thing I want to teach you is that readers find that when they want to . . . it often helps to . . ."). Then show them, by returning to a part of a familiar class read-aloud.

- Coach kids to try doing the new work themselves, perhaps leaving them with a scaffold like a short list of sentence starters or a chart of steps to follow.

- Let kids know you will check in again soon, and at that time, follow up.

Small-group work will be more powerful if you do smaller bouts of it across time than if you have one gigantic small-group session every few weeks. It helps to work with a particular small group for around ten minutes, two or three times a week, for a week or two, rather than working with that group once every week or two, each time for half an hour. The advantage of more frequent short meetings is that you can channel children to do some work related to the group between your meetings. This allows the group work to influence their reading for broader stretches of time.

There Is No One Way to Lead Small Groups. The Best Is to Draw from a Repertoire of Possible Small Groups.

I encourage you to develop a repertoire of ways of working with small groups. Native Alaskans, lore has it, have twenty-six words for *snow*. They're such experts on snow that they don't think of all that white stuff as just one monolithic thing. And I'm convinced that with increasing expertise, you, also, can realize that all your small-group work need not fit into one template or bear a single label. In fact, for your small-group teaching to be responsive, you need to outgrow any feeling that every small group proceeds in the same way. If you have been trained that every small group begins with you distributing copies of the same text to a small group of matched readers, then you giving a text introduction, followed by a time in which readers each read that text while you circle among them, listening to one child and then another read aloud while you coach into each individual's reading, you need to understand that yes, indeed, that is one way that small groups can go. Many people refer to that format as guided reading.

The most important thing to say about small-group work is, "Do it!"

But know that other teachers do entirely different things under the name of guided reading; it is a term that has vastly different interpretations in one school and another. In some communities, guided reading entails children gathering, carrying whatever book they are in the midst of reading, and the teacher then talks a bit about a strategy—perhaps, for example, the teacher points out that some dialogue is untagged and shows kids that when the text doesn't say who is talking, the reader mentally adds that information in, keeping track always of who is talking. Then the teacher channels the group members to continue reading wherever they left off in their book, and the teacher rotates among the group members, asking each to read aloud a bit when the teacher is there, with the teacher coaching into that reading.

Then, too, there are classrooms in which teachers interpret guided reading to be what others might call a "book club" or a "literature circle." Yet other classrooms think of guided reading as (I hate to say it) round-robin reading, or unison reading, or a shared textbook.

This suggests that it is important to understand that there is no one way to lead guided reading groups or to lead small groups. You have choices. One thing we know for certain about young readers is they are not all the same! At a conference at Teachers College, the reading researcher Richard Allington recently reported that most teachers have only one format for their small groups. The irony is that we work with small groups instead of the whole class, precisely so that we can tailor our teaching to our students.

There are abundant ways in which you can work with small groups, and this is especially true because this is a format in which you will sometimes work in out-of-the-box ways, trying something bold that you have never tried before just on the off-chance it might help. After all, your small-group instruction will be your forum for working with students for whom in-the-box sorts of teaching may not have done the job.

For example, think about all the ways in which you teach reading to your whole class. Consider whether each of those ways of teaching reading might be done in small groups. Presumably you read aloud to your whole class and engage kids in accountable talk conversations. Why not lead small groups that help kids needing extra support learning how to participate well in that work? Then, too, if you teach third-graders, you probably engage the whole class in shared reading, orchestrating the class to read a text aloud chorally, in unison. Wouldn't some students benefit from small-group shared reading? Then, too, might you engage small groups of students in word study?

My point is that I think it is helpful for you to imagine a wide repertoire of sorts of small groups.

PLANNING A SEQUENCE OF SMALL GROUPS

I think it is helpful for you to imagine small groups as occurring across a sequence of days, building off each other, with you deliberately removing some of the scaffolds as the group becomes more practiced.

For example, you might plan a sequence of small groups to support kids reading texts that are a bit harder than those they have been reading on their own. For your first session, you may tell readers that you believe they are ready to handle texts that are a notch harder than those they have been reading, and you may then give a text introduction to what they will be reading in sync with each other. Let's imagine it is an article. In your text introduction, instead of simply telling them about the article they'll read, you will want to do so in ways that show them how to orient themselves to future articles. So you'll say, "Let's preview this article, as readers do, to get ready to read." Then you might say, "I usually look first to see if there are headings and introductory comments, don't you? Let's look." In that way, you walk kids through the sources of whatever orienting comments you will give them. You might then say, "The other thing I do before I read is think about some of the challenging words I'm apt to encounter," and you could show kids how you skim for those words, and that would then set you up to explain a few of them. Your introduction will provide more information than kids could have extrapolated themselves, but my point is you do this work in a way that sets kids up to do it themselves. You will probably also want to let readers know about a way in which the texts they are tending to read these days will pose challenges, and help them with one or two of those challenges. For example, you may want to help them integrate text boxes and illustrations into their reading of paragraphs. Then kids can get started reading, either while you listen to one child after another, coaching into their reading, or while you check the rest of the class.

The next day, when you reconvene this group, you will not want to provide as much scaffolding. You might ask kids to preview the text themselves, constructing their own approximation of a text introduction, with you chiming in to coach or to help as needed. By the third session, you might set readers up to work individually, on their own, and then to teach each other what they noticed, with you again coaching in. In that way, you go from heavily supported guided reading to more lightly supported.

Your small groups can support higher-level comprehension, not just progress up the ladder of text complexity. For example, you might gather a small group to help kids mine a text for its themes. On that first day, to offer lots of support, you could set kids up to listen as you read aloud a picture book, suggesting it helps to listen for repetition that feels significant or for instances when an object or a part of the setting seems to mean more than at first meets the eye. In that case, as you read aloud, you may alter your tone or pause and give a meaningful look at kids when you reach such a spot. The group could pause to talk in the midst of the read-aloud, with you providing sentence prompts. Then suggest that kids continue this work in their independent books, taking some sentence prompts with them, maybe on bookmarks. The next time that small group meets, you might suggest students read aloud their own books to each other, with the reader and the listener again attending to significant repetition. Another time the group meets, kids could teach each other what they found in their independent books, using rubrics to assess and coach into each other's work. Once kids begin to be more proficient, you could send another group to interview, researching and studying what they had learned to do, and then trying the same work.

Here's another possibility. You want to teach students that when they predict, their predictions need to be based on the details of the text they have already read. You reread the last bit of the book you have read aloud to the class, and show them that when they predict, they need to draw on details from earlier in the text. You do this just a bit, and then you get them to try it with the same book. Then you channel readers to read on in their books, and when they come to a spot where they can do some prediction, to stop and jot that prediction, remembering to do what you just demonstrated. As students work on this, you move from one to another, coaching into their work.

As you plan your small groups, it is helpful to anticipate using the gradual release of responsibility model to progress from heavy to light scaffolding as learners become more proficient in the strategy you are teaching. The concept of scaffolded instruction was first used by Wood et al. (1976) to talk about children's language development. Referring to the temporary structures that are installed and eventually removed from around a building under construction, they suggested that by varying the amounts of scaffolding, learners could be successful. This is an important principle of teaching. Teachers provide learners with maximum support for something that is just beyond their reach, and then gradually remove that support so learners can function with increasing autonomy (Pearson and Gallagher 1983).

Approach any small-group work as an ongoing research project. You are continually researching the children, their needs, and their response to your instruction.

Bringing a research stance and a sense of innovation to your small groups will ensure they are joyful, energetic parts of your children's reading lives and your teaching days.

Partnerships
LAUNCHING AND SUSTAINING POWERFUL READING PARTNERSHIPS

Partnerships are a fundamental part of a reading workshop classroom. Few of us read books in total isolation. Instead, we note passages we want to share and bring our marked-up books together with our peers for thought-provoking conversations. We read articles on our smart phones and then reference the most fascinating tidbits from those articles over dinner. We share favorite books with friends we know will love them. It's hard for us to keep our thoughts about books to ourselves. We get excited about ideas gleaned from reading, and we can't wait to share, discuss, analyze, and stretch those ideas to form new ideas.

It's important to create those same situations for the readers in your class. To start, you'll want to match all your students with reading partners, and you'll want those partners to be strategically selected. Often, students are matched with partners at a similar reading level, so they can swap books. You might also consider the kinds of books kids like to read, their habits, and their social bonds. Partnership work, after all, is practice for being study partners in high school and college. Within a nonfiction reading unit, however, you might partner students based on interest, since students can read about any given topic at a variety of reading levels. Then, too, you'll want those partnerships to be long lasting. Many teachers keep these partnerships together for at least the duration of the unit, even longer if the partnerships are going well.

Whenever possible, you'll want partners to be reading the same book, series, genre, or topic. It's easier to talk about books when partners read the same thing. Conversations will be at a higher level because they don't need to include much retelling. There are multiple copies of books included in your Classroom Library to facilitate this. However, if you find you don't have enough pairs of titles for partners to read the same books, you might encourage readers to be swap-book partnerships. That is, both readers could be reading two books from the EllRay Jakes series, with one reading *EllRay Jakes and the Beanstalk* and another reading *EllRay Jakes Is Magic*. When they're finished, they can swap. This ensures that at least half the time, children will be talking about books that their partner knows well, and regardless, they are sharing in books with the same characters and overall plot structure. If one reader is ready to proceed to more challenging texts before his partner is, you may need to finesse this by creating temporary triads.

Another reason to create triads is to help English language learners. For these students, partnerships (or triads) often contain a more proficient speaker of English and a less proficient speaker. For newcomers, the partnerships may be language-based—for example, two speakers of Urdu working together.

Once your students are matched in reading partnerships and books, you'll want to consider the times in which they can work with their partners. Many teachers choose to have partners sit near each other. They'll regularly ask students to turn-and-talk with their partners across the minilesson, saying things like "Partner 1 can you tell Partner 2 what you're noticing about character development in your reading today?" Partners might work together for a few minutes during the mid-workshop, which comes midway through the lesson. Then, the reading workshop will usually end with five minutes of time left for partner conversations.

Partners can do a variety of work together. You might visit the Teachers College Reading and Writing Project's Vimeo site, at www.vimeo.com/tcrwp, to see videos of partnerships in action. You might even decide to play video clips for your students to set them up to work with partners in similar ways. In the videos, notice how the students move beyond retelling what happened in the text, and instead, how they engage each other by zooming in on powerful parts in the book, acting out those parts, and discussing the significance of them.

The powerful reading partnerships you foster in your classroom will lay the foundation for book club work later in the year.

To Support Your Students' Reading Lives, Energize Your Own Reading

In the end, the best thing you can do to nourish and energize your students' independent reading lives is to nourish and energize your own. We all need to make the time to burrow under the covers and read that tantalizing book, to read the newspaper, to track down the picture book we adored when we were six, to order the new Pulitzer Prize winner or the latest sleazy beach book. We need to be adult readers, and we need to know the books in our Classroom Libraries, too. Having read these books, you can authentically pull alongside to say, "Did you just finish *Harry Potter and the Half-Blood Prince*?!? Can you believe that . . . ?" We need to do this because, by reading, we layer our experience and develop greater breadth and depth to draw on in our teaching. But we need to do this most of all, because when we love reading, when we ourselves draw power and strength and peace from reading, we educate our students' imagination about what their own world of reading can be.

③ Book Clubs

An Introduction to Book Clubs

When you unpack the books that constitute your library—or even when you see the available choices when ordering portions of these libraries—you'll see that we've set lots of books aside for book clubs. For kids at every level, you'll see shelves with four copies of twelve titles. (We would have offered more books, but you probably have several copies of books to add to any of these book club shelves.)

The decision to include multiple copies of books makes a statement. After all, we could have introduced you to forty-eight distinct fantasy books, instead of channeling you to get four copies of twelve titles. So why, you may be asking, are book clubs such a big deal?

It comes down to the power of *relationships*. Think about any time you have been glad to work hard on a project. If you pause to think, "Why did I like doing that work?" your answer may revolve around the people with whom you worked. In *A Place Called School*, John Goodlad reports on interviews with thousands of kids. When he asked them, "What's the best part of school for you?" almost every child answered, "My friends." And the truth is, if you and I are happy with our work, the best part of it is the relationships.

For reading to be "hot" for your kids, you need to do everything you can to create relationships around books, and book clubs are the perfect way to do that. Alan Purves has said, "It takes two to read a book," and for many of us, the books we remember best are those we have shared. Think for a moment about the conversations that happen on the way out of a movie theater: "Can you believe that ending?" "Wow, I hope there's a sequel!" "I thought that doctor character was really strange—why was he in the film anyhow?" What a great day it will be when your kids talk in similar ways about books!

And they will. You'll hear conversations about books spill over into the lunchroom and the schoolyard, as students share their latest thinking about their club book and question each other's conclusions. You'll see kids set up play dates to watch movies based on their club books and arrange trips to the library to secure later titles in the series.

Perhaps most importantly, being in a book club at a young age sets students up for a life of book club membership. In a society where 85% of students report they won't read for pleasure after high school, it's imperative that we do all we can to create reading structures and routines that extend beyond our classrooms. A child who experiences being part of a book club will draw on those experiences fondly as an adult and may try to re-create them. When you set up book clubs, you're setting up lifelong readers.

Planning for Book Clubs: The Nuts and Bolts

What is a book club?

Simply put, a book club is a group of readers, usually four, who read books roughly in sync with each other. Often clubs read a series of books together that share a common genre—mystery, historical fiction, fantasy—or they read a collection of disparate books with a common lens—thinking about interpretation, learning about shared social issues across the book.

How will you form clubs?

When forming book clubs, you may start by having students write you a note telling you the people they believe would be good book club partners for them. To do that, children think about peers who read similar books, at a similar pace, and who work well together. You won't please everyone, but you'll probably be able to consider many of their wishes as you create book clubs. Usually the clubs contain two sets of reading partners. You'll be careful to group students who read close to the same level of text complexity. Clubs provide support to readers, so it is not uncommon for teachers to use this structure to support kids moving to books that are a notch harder than those they have been reading, allowing the club to double as a guided reading group. It is also common for a club to involve a few kids who have been reading a particular level of text complexity for a while, and another child who is new to that level.

How will book clubs get started?

Say you decide to have your kids working in fantasy book clubs. You've got the books—forty-eight on our shelf and multiple copies of a few other books that you may round up to add to that shelf. Now what?

One of your first decisions will be whether you want to plunge right in, saying something to your kids like, "Boys and girls, starting tomorrow, you will each be in a club of readers, making your way through a sequence of shared fantasy books." Or alternatively, do you want to ease your kids into this work? If you decide on the latter, you could read aloud a fantasy book to kids who are sitting with others whom you imagine will eventually comprise a club. During turn-and-talks at key moments throughout the read-aloud, you can ask these groups of kids (nascent clubs) to talk together about the book. This, of course, will make conversations among members of a club much easier than they would be if the children were reading and jotting about their club books at home and then gathering just to talk, as will happen

For reading to be "hot" for your kids, you need to do everything you can to create relationships around books, and book clubs are the perfect way to do that.

soon. If you are reading aloud just prior to the talking time, you needn't worry over whether some kids may not have done the required reading to prepare for the club. You can also select pause points at particularly talk-worthy moments in the text, and if added help is needed, you can even launch the conversation among the whole class before saying, "Continue to talk about this in your club."

One advantage of launching clubs this way is that as you watch kids talking together, you can then do some social engineering ("Raymond is absent, will you join this club instead?") that can end up making the eventual book club more successful. Another way to ease into clubs is to launch one book club at a time. If you choose that option, while most of the class reads books that have been chosen independently, you could gather four readers who you hope would be eager to constitute a new club. You could give that club support to get it off to a strong start before launching a second club.

However you choose to organize and begin clubs in your room, you will want to feel comfortable giving your kids a quick keynote about the importance of book clubs. You might nudge them to think of a time in their lives when they were a part of a club or a team: a soccer club, a karate club, a chess club, a video game club. What made those clubs work well, or not so well?

Supporting Book Clubs so They Go Well— and Anticipating Challenges

In most classrooms, teachers decide to have all the clubs meet at the same time on the same days—that is, perhaps Tuesdays and Fridays are book club meeting days, with Monday, Wednesday, and Thursday for independent reading, partner conversations, and writing about reading. Because all the clubs are talking at the same time, this means that club conversations need to be sustained mostly without you there to make this happen. Most club conversations last for about twenty minutes. If you worry that students won't be able to sustain conversation, you can always start with shorter meetings. You can also make it clear that once book club members have run out of steam, they can resume reading their books. You may also channel less experienced readers (and talkers) to meet more often for shorter times. For most readers, it helps to have a few days between club meetings so they have time to gather steam before they meet again.

One way or another, you'll want to convey that for a club to be successful, kids need to take seriously their obligations to each other. Being a good club member means coming to the meetings, having done the reading (and the writing about reading) that club members agreed to do before the discussion. You will have expectations around the volume of reading and of writing about reading that kids do between club meetings, varying by grade level and club. You might expect third-graders to come to their mystery book clubs with a few Post-it notes or an updated chart of suspects, while you might expect fifth-graders to come to an interpretation book club with new insights jotted in page-long entries. What matters most is that your readers don't come to a club meeting empty-handed.

Clubs often begin with one reader sharing an idea, and then other students respond to that idea, for as long as it makes sense. Other clubs may start by glancing at everyone's jots, quickly gleaning common topics and overlapping ideas, and then picking one as a jumping-off point for a discussion. Some clubs routinely start conversations by returning to their previous conversation and talk about what they thought, noticed, or wondered as they read in the wake of that last conversation. Teach club members that before a club conversation ends, members need to decide on the chapters they'll be reading and to decide on the topic they will be thinking and writing about. A club might decide to track a theory they came up with about a main character, flagging scenes that fit with or go against the theory. Or they might decide to make sense of the complex world of their fantasy novel, building a map of the place as they read and making notes about characters' responses to different places. If all the club members think and write about the same question or topic, then their club conversation is more likely to go well.

Coaching and Conferring with Clubs

When you stop by a club to listen to the talk, it's easy to take over that conversation without intending to. You drop by a club for a moment, interject an idea, and before you know it, the kids are all looking at *you* while sharing their ideas, instead of directing their thoughts to the group. So you don't inadvertently slip into that way of interacting with a club, we recommend you rely on three main methods to strengthen club talk. You might temporarily join a club, functioning as a proficient partner by doing the work that a good club member/reader would do, and carry the ball for at least a bit of the conversation. You might model how to build on a club member's ideas, instead of leaping in to share your ideas. Or, you might show students how you reference passages from the book to make your conversation more text-based.

Additionally, you can whisper in lean prompts to lift the level of what club members do. "Find a page that shows that," you might say. "Did you understand what he said? If not, ask him to explain." These prompts keep the conversation going among your students—and they help lift the level of the conversation.

You can also pause the club, do a bit of research, and then give a compliment and a teaching point. You might listen for a bit, then say, "I'm trying to understand how your club usually works. What is the big goal you're trying to accomplish now in your talk?" This allows you to see if the talk you overheard matches what students intended. At that point, you could give a tip. Perhaps you suggest the readers make a tool to guide their talk, such as a timeline, to help them keep track of events, or a suspect list that could help them collect clues to help solve a mystery.

Another way to elevate the level of a club is to have students observe a model club. If you have access to the Units of Study for Teaching Reading, you might want to look at Grade 5, Unit 1, *Interpretation Book Clubs*. In Session 10, fifth-graders watch a video of kids engaged in a book club conversation about *My Name Is María Isabel*, paying attention to how club members exchange ideas and revise and elevate their thinking about a book.

You'll be floored by how quickly kids will take on the work of book clubs. Clubs offer a welcome change of pace to independent reading and a venue for children to discuss ideas in a safe, comfortable space with peers. As you continue to confer and coach into clubs, you'll see students delve more deeply into a shared topic, disagree with each other more willingly, and self-reflect more critically. It's the kind of work we dream of for our kids—and the best part is, they take ownership over it, too.

Nonfiction Book Clubs

Of course, you won't want to reserve the excitement of book clubs just for fiction books. You can also group kids in similar ways when teaching nonfiction units. You might divide students into research groups by interest, with one group studying extreme sports, another studying animals in captivity, and a third studying how to help the environment. Or, if your class is engaged in a more focused research study, you might offer students a choice of subtopics. For example, if you are reading about how to help the environment, you could have one group of students studying the pros/cons of recycling, another group studying water conservation, a third group reading about garbage and how to create less waste, and a fourth group studying how to build greener buildings. Studying issues within a group allows students to consider these issues more deeply, revise their thinking, raise questions, and even debate. The students studying recycling, for example, might debate that issue within their club. Or, you might set up the students to debate across clubs. Members of the recycling and water conservation clubs might debate: "What is most important way to help the environment: recycle or save water?"

Videos on the TCRWP Site

For more information about clubs, visit the Teachers College Reading and Writing Project Vimeo site, where you'll see some videos capturing club conversations. For example, in the video "A Research Club Discusses the Issue of Bottled Water," students studying bottled water discuss the issue with their research team (see https://vimeo.com/145312922, search terms: video research club bottled water). You might notice how students come prepared for their conversation and regularly reference the work in their notebooks.